Neuschwa...
An 'Exploring ~~Castles~~ Travel Guide

Updated: April 2016
Edd Morris
www.exploring-castles.com

Cover/above image: Shutterstock/Sean Pavone

ISBN-13: 978-1530754014
ISBN-10: 1530754011

Please note that I've made every effort to try and ensure that information in this book is accurate. This edition was published in April 2016.

If there's anything I've missed, I'm happy to answer your questions. Go to www.exploring-castles.com and choose the 'Contact Me' option.

Legally, I must tell you that I can't make any warranty about the content of this guide. Information is provided on an 'as-is' basis, and I disclaim all liability arising from the use of information herein.

Please note that this guide is an unofficial work with no connection to Neuschwanstein Castle.

Table of Contents

1.0 An Introduction

1.1 Neuschwanstein: An Introduction

Neuschwanstein Castle is one of Europe's most popular tourist attractions. A marvel of creativity, eccentricity and frenzied imagination, it's a mock-Medieval castle built against a spectacular Alpine backdrop. Neuschwanstein is located in the village of Hohenschwangau, in Bavaria, Germany - on the borders of Austria.

The castle was the work of King Ludwig II - one of those European monarchs who has been elevated to near-mythological status over the years. Despite being born just 15 years before the American Civil War began, this eccentric king of Bavaria was obsessed with tales of Medieval chivalry and fantasy.

So, whilst the rest of Europe was racing full-pelt towards the World Wars of the twentieth century, King Ludwig was gazing longingly at times gone by.

Inspired by the operas of Wagner, and dreaming of knights and maidens of yore, King Ludwig poured his energy - and vast sums of money - into creating a series of eccentric castles studded around Bavaria. The castles were an outlet for his preoccupation with a fantasy world - distracting him from the pain and failure of his faltering rule, and his difficult personal life.

Of all his bizarre creations - from the indoor-wave machine in the grotto of Linderhof Palace, to his recreation of Versailles on German soil - Neuschwanstein is most famous of all, and has achieved iconic status.

In the words of Ludwig, Neuschwastein was intended to be "heilig und unnahbar" - sacred yet out of reach. Vast yet delicate, ostentatious yet somewhat tragic, Neuschwanstein teeters on an Alpine precipice, surrounded by truly jaw-dropping natural beauty. Its broad bulk is capped with an array of swirling turrets, and its lime-white walls add a touch of palatial elegance.

An aerial view of the castle. Shutterstock /WGXC

The spectacular exterior of the castle more than matches the extravagant interior decor. From the vast throne-room, dripping with gold leaf, to the over-ornate carved wooden bedroom, the sheer decadence of Neuschwanstein's furnishing is really something to behold.

However, there's a certain sadness that lends the outrageous decor a grounding in reality. The truth is that the castle was never finished - many of the rooms beyond the reach of tourists are bare cinder-blocks, and many of the turrets were truncated from their original height. The reason? King Ludwig was deposed in 1886 on the grounds of insanity. His castle was never completed - and he died in mysterious circumstances just days later.

King Ludwig poured his hopes, dreams and aspirations into Neuschwanstein - a secret mountain hideaway for a tortured, isolated soul. There's a cruel irony that millions of tourists each year now take a trip to the castle to catch a glimpse of its magical outline - and each hang their own dreams, plans, and aspirations onto this real-life fairytale.

Thank you for buying this book. You'll find it divided into two sections - the first part deals describes the context and history of Neuschwanstein and King Ludwig, and the second part deals with the practicalities of trip planning.

I hope you find the information useful and interesting - and that your visit to Neuschwanstein is a brilliant one.

Edd Morris
London, UK. (2016)

1.2 To Start: A Myth Buster

Shutterstock / Santi Rodriguez

Before we get going properly, let's dispel a few rumours and misconceptions about Neuschwanstein. Being one of the world's most popular tourist hotspots, there's been a fair bit of misinformation written about the place.

The first thing really is a piece of trivia. King Ludwig would never have referred to the place as *Neuschwanstein*. The castle only gained its contemporary name after Ludwig's death. He knew it as New Hohenschwangau Castle - an allusion to the rebuilding of his father's castle of Hohenschwangau, which lay just across the valley. After his death, the castle began to be known by the more romantic Neuschwanstein (New Swan Stone).

The second misconception is more important. Neuschwanstein is frequently perceived to be the ideal Medieval castle. It's a strange misunderstanding, as there's nothing authentically Medieval about the place at all - the first foundations were laid three years after the American Civil War ended.

Neuschwanstein Castle, then, is as authentically Medieval as Cinderella's Castle in Walt Disney World. Don't mistake my point, though, as being cynical or critical - I'm just trying to emphasise the chronology of the place.

So if Neuschwanstein isn't a Medieval fairytale, what is it? Well, it's a work of historicism - an artistic movement that drew inspiration from times past. Historicism exaggerated and accentuated historic styles - a modern take on past architecture. By this count, Neuschwanstein is an over-perfect rendering of a fantastic Medieval dream. Both its exterior and interior evoke an idealised vision of Medieval times which never truly existed - almost like a film set, you might say.

And that's almost certainly down to the fact that Neuschwanstein was, in the main, was designed by a theatre set designer, Christian Jank. He devised the place for maximum aesthetic impact. Rather like the other castles of King Ludwig (such as Herrenchiemsee or Linderhof), the setting, contours and colours of the castle were laboriously chosen to maximise the visual impact upon any bystander.

This leads onto my final point about the castle - how to really interpret and appreciate the place. There's no doubt that Neuschwanstein tip-toes the line between good taste and camp kitsch, and there have been plenty of critics lining up to debunk the place as a crude and classless expression of a monarch with more access to money than sense.

I'd disagree. My viewpoint is that, to appreciate Neuschwanstein, you need to see it as being the life's work and ambition of King Ludwig. Seen through the prism of his eccentricity - his obsessions, his dreams, and his fears - the place makes much more sense. Rather than a gaudy, touristy, fairground attraction, I believe that Neuschwanstein really is a 'castle in the sky' - the physical expression of the bizarre dreams and aspirations of one man with who had the means to build them.

2.0 Exploring Neuschwanstein Castle

2.1 Neuschwanstein: Conception and Construction

In 1869, construction began upon King Ludwig II's dream castle: the palace that we now know as Neuschwanstein. But it had been a long and convoluted path to begin building: and, as we know all too well, it was a project which would never be completed.

It appears that Ludwig had always harboured an interest in the ruins of the two castles which lay in sight of his childhood summer home of Hohenschwangau (see p94). The decaying remnants of Vorderhohenschwangau and Hinterhohenschwangau castles hinted at a Medieval grandeur, long lost. When hiking up to the ruins, he got a glimpse of a spectacular view across the Alps and the adjacent Alpsee: and likely sensed that this would be a spectacular spot to build his own castle.

In the late 1860s, Ludwig began to give this niggling idea a little more attention. Ludwig was an idealistic young king who would be forever blighted by one misjudgement - backing Austria (the losing side) within the Austro-Prussian war of 1866. The consequence of this mis-step (and the subsequent formation of the German Empire) meant that Bavaria was reduced from an independent kingdom to minor state of Prussia. Almost overnight, his powers as a king were stripped from him: his significance virtually became ceremonial alone.

From that point onwards, it appears that Ludwig retreated into himself. He became obsessed with creating and inhabiting a fantasy world of Medieval romance, where the power of the king was absolute (see p27). Rather than concern himself with governing a state, he set about building castles in the sky.

Christian Jank, a theatrical stage-designer, was responsible for the design of Neuschwanstein, and an architect named Eduard Riedel had the unenviable job of converting Jank's drawings - and Ludwig's increasingly unrealistic ideas - into a practical construction plan. Ludwig maintained a vice-like grip on the project, and the castle cycled through two further architects: each, presumably, more patient than the last.

In 1868, the remains on the two medieval castles on site were unceremoniously blown up; and in 1869, the first stone of Neuschwanstein was laid. Ludwig had settled upon an elaborate Romanesque design inspired by the works of Wagner (see below): but, even with construction underway, Ludwig's grand plans remained fluid: vast sections, most notably the Throne Room, were conceived later in the process.

A photo of Neuschwanstein during construction. Taken by Johannes Bernhard between 1882 and 1885.

In June 1872, the first building to be completed - and the least coherent structure, when viewing the castle today - was the red-brick gatehouse. An apartment was fashioned at the top of the building, so that King Ludwig could keep a very close eye on the construction of the remainder of the castle. (Until that time, he'd just been able to spy across the valley from Hohenschwangau - through a golden telescope).

The construction of Neuschwanstein would have been an engineering nightmare. The narrow, remote cliff edge was (and remains) unstable; and transporting materials, including hundreds of tonnes of bright white limestone cladding, proved a logistic challenge. At the height of the building project, more than 300 men were involved in the project, and some of the most modern technologies - including a steel frame support for the throne room - were utilised in rendering this Medieval fantasy into reality.

The original grand plans for Neuschwanstein included more than 200 rooms, with little coherent plan as what so much space would actually be used for. The bulk of the accommodations were planned for the Palas - the largest and most visible section of the castle.

The five-storey Palas is connected to the Gatehouse via the Knight's House - a long, corridor-like building with an impressive arched gallery. A smaller building - the 'Bower' - adjoins the Palas on the southeastern aspect. All these buildings crowd around a courtyard. A profusion of towers - mostly decorative - asymmetrically stud the structures; the tallest of which is 213 ft (65m).

Construction of the Palas began in 1872, and the building 'topped out' in 1880. Of the 15 rooms that would ever be completed, a good amount of interior decoration was finished by 1884, enabling King Ludwig to - tentatively - move into the castle. At his death in 1886, however, Neuschwanstein would have still been a building site.

Although the majority of the Palas exterior was compete, the associated structures - including the Knight's House and Bower - were little more than foundations.

After Ludwig's death, at the discretion of the Regent Luitpold, both the Knight's House and Bower were built - albeit at a much smaller scale than detailed on Ludwig's last plans, and without the same degree of elaborate external decoration. (As an example, the Knight's House was meant to be flanked with stone trees; and a female figure was planned to be carved into the Bower).

Most significantly, at the far end of the upper courtyard, Ludwig had planned a gigantic stone keep - a vast tower 300ft (90m) high, which would have emerged from the nave of a small chapel. This edifice would never be built, and you can glimpse the proposed foundations of this mega-structure when you pass through the courtyard on the tour.

Under Regent Luitpold, there was also a drive to decorate some of the internal rooms to completion. Conversely, he decided to abandon sections where decorations had not yet begun - such as the fabled Moorish Hall. Today, many of the chambers in the castle remain empty, and tantalisingly off limits for tourists.

2.2 Themes of Neuschwanstein

Certain themes crop up again and again when touring Neuschwanstein: the influence of Wagner's work; staging and theatricality; the quest for purity; and the role of the king in Medieval times. Here are the key themes to look out for.

The Work of Richard Wagner

Ludwig was obsessed with the operatic work of Wagner, and became his chief financial benefactor. Due to Ludwig's patronage,

Wagner went on to write some of the most noted operas of his career, which are still enjoyed by audiences across the world.

The two men had a truly synergistic relationship, and spurred each other on to greatness. Neuschwanstein was designed to embody some of Wagner's works - Tannhäuser, Lohengrin and Parsifal.

The Legend of Parzival/The Grail King

Parzival was a character of German Medieval legend - a knight who battled and overcame sin because of his dedication to religious faith and purity. His inner strength lead him to the Castle of the Holy Grail, Montsalvat, where his inner strength transformed him into the Grail King.

Wagner's last operatic work was Parsifal and it was a nickname that he gave to Ludwig when the pair were exchanging letters. Pious and self-tortured Ludwig was also obsessed with the knight, and the Throne Room of Neuschwanstein represents the Hall of the Holy Grail from the Medieval legend.

The Swan, and the Knight Lohengrin

The image of the swan was already embedded within the Bavarian Royal Family from Ludwig's childhood. His father, Maximilian, had adopted the swan as an unofficial Royal motif - the regal bird was associated with the area surrounding the castle ('Hohenschwangau' effectively means 'High Swan Country'). In addition to this, Ludwig was also intrigued by the Medieval legend of Lohengrin.

Lohengrin was the son of Parzival, and was another pious knight. He was beckoned to a troubled kingdom, and travelled there, pulled on the back of a boat pulled by a swan. Despite his good deeds in the troubled land, he was condemned to eternal solitude after disclosing the answer to a forbidden question. He was the inspiration behind another of Wager's works, *Lohengrin*.

You'll notice an entire alcove dedicated to the image of the swan in the castle living room.

Wagner's Opera Tannhäuser, and The Medieval Minsterel's Contest

Minnesingers were Medieval German poets and song-writers - troubadours, if you like. Tannhäuser was a Medieval knight who travelled from castle to castle, singing chaste songs of perfect love. He participated in numerous singing concerts, including one in Wartburg Castle, in 1207.

However, his beautiful voice - which won numerous contests - became his downfall. Venus was so attracted to him that she beckoned him to her - and seduced him into carnal love. Entirely seduced by sin, his songs within his next concert became filled with lyrics depicting the pleasures of sensual love. This incurred the wrath of God, who exiled him to wander the Alps forever.

The mythology of Tannhäuser was the inspiration for Wagner's opera of the same name, and the Singer's Hall in the castle was intended as the physical embodiment of part of the story.

2.3 A Tour by Words: A Written Guide to Neuschwanstein Castle

Your tour of Neuschwanstein is likely to be a little rushed: a consequence of the vast numbers of tourists visiting the castle every year. If you'd like a little more detail, here's a run-through of each of the rooms which constitute the present route.

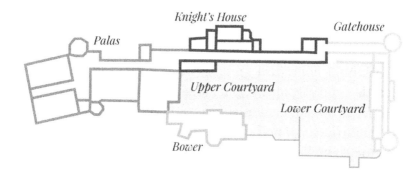

A ground plan of Neuschwanstein, demonstrating the different sections which form the lower floor of the castle.

The Approach to the Castle

Whereas most of Neuschwanstein Castle is coated in an attractive white limestone, the red-brick finish of the Gatehouse stands in stark contrast to the remainder of the castle.

The Bavarian Royal Coat of Arms is chiselled into the stone above the portcullis; and two bartizans (projecting corner turrets) flank the entranceway.

The gatehouse was realised by Eduard von Riedel, the first of three architects involved in the project. Von Riedel's designs were a little too prosaic for Ludwig's liking, and so he was shifted to other jobs.

Despite this (or perhaps because of it), the gatehouse was finished to time in 1872. Above the entrance doorway are a series of rooms (not accessible to today's visitors): Ludwig stayed here when he visited the castle, and watched the engineering work for the remainder of the palace. The downstairs rooms were intended to be stables.

The Upper and Lower Courtyard

Visitors are held within the lower section of the castle courtyard whilst waiting for their allotted tour time.

Within the courtyard, you can see the Palas - the body of the castle - directly ahead. But almost everything else you see in the courtyard wasn't completed as to Ludwig's plans: the Bower, to the left side, is much smaller than planned. The Knight's House, to the right, lacks the elaborate external carvings that the king dreamed of.

Most significantly, Ludwig had planned a small chapel and a 300ft tower ('The Keep') - the foundations of which are visible today. Due to his death, neither would be completed.

Knight's House

Nowadays, the long building on the north-westerly aspect is used as an access pathway into the main Palas: a place to collect and corral tour groups. Although this building is ostensibly referred to as the Knight's House, it was also envisaged by King Ludwig to fulfil ancillary functions, such as servant's quarters.

The tour guide will lead you through these passageways, and up spiral stairs, to the Palas. Note that the furnished areas are only on the third and fourth floors: the remaining areas remain incomplete (or used for modern stores or tourist shops).

Inside the Palas: The Entrance Hall

The beauty of the entrance-hall to the castle has been lost to temporary barriers and queuing structures, designed to expedite touring groups around Neuschwanstein's innards.

Compared to the rest of the castle, the room is relatively understated - using dark wood and restful colours, perhaps to accentuate the wild decor of much of the rest of the castle.

The paintings on the wall depict classical stories from the Old Norse saga of Edda. Much of Wagner's work was inspired by Norse myth, which helps explain the choice of decoration. The impressive vaulted ceiling gives way to two marble entrances: one to the Royal Apartments, and one to the Throne Room.

The Throne Room

Undoubtedly one of the most arresting rooms of the entire castle, the two storey, 43ft high throne room drips with gold leaf. The over-riding theme of the room is the legitimacy of a King's Divine Right to rule - an incongruous obsession in rapidly industrializing Europe.

Imagery within the room depicts the twelve apostles, alongside the six holy kings. More pictures of saints adorn the walls, and the vast mosaic on the floor depicts God's creations - the varied plants and animals of Earth.

The vast golden chandelier, which rather dominates the room, weighs more than a ton, and was apparently designed in the style of a Byzantine crown. It's lowered twice a year, rather ceremoniously, to allow for cleaning.

Marble steps lead up to a vast platform, that's further accentuated by a dramatic, golden dome. This would have been the place for the throne - but you'll notice that the throne isn't there.

A prosaic explanation would have been that there was no time to finish the throne before Ludwig's death. However, Christopher Mcintosh, in his book *The Swan King*, argues that the throne was never intended to be included. Micintosh's argument is that the Throne Room symbolically represents the sanctuary of the Holy

Grail on earth. The throne would represent the Holy Grail itself - which will never be found, and so will always remain absent.

The Throne Room. Photo taken 1886.

It's a powerful idea - that there's an intentional incompleteness at the heart of Neuschwanstein. This incompleteness illustrates Ludwig's understanding of the imperfection of earthly life.

The Dining Room

The Dining Room's restful ambience is due to its luxuriant construction of carved, dark oak. Note the size of the table, though: by the time the plans for the room were being finalised, Ludwig was firmly retreating into a solitary existence, and there's barely room for a dining companion.

A state-of-the-art electric bell system was added to the room, so Ludwig could summon a servant whenever he needed (retreating into isolation, he objected to actually having to see servants within the castle).

The walls of the room depict the legend of the Medieval Minnesingers, who performed at a contest in Wartburg Castle in 1207. This contest was the inspiration behind Wagner's opera the Tannhäuser, and can be glimpsed again within the Singer's Hall (at the end of the tour).

The Bedroom

Possibly the most ornate of all rooms, King Ludwig's bedroom is said to have taken 14 woodcarvers more than four years to finish. The central motif of the room is Wagner's opera Tristan and Isolde - characters from which are studded throughout the carvings.

A semi-secret door through one of the carved walls would have allowed servants to pass through the room unobtrusively while the king was elsewhere.

A wash-stand in the side of the room enjoyed flowing water, tapped ingeniously from a stream which runs just above the castle. The water would have flown out through the spectacular, silver-plated swan which is still present upon the wash-stand.

The Chapel

The Chapel esposes another of King Ludwig's obsessions - King Louis XI of France. Louis XI is France's only canonised monarch, who ruled in - unsurprisingly - Medieval times. The chapel depicts numerous scenes from King Louis' life, elevated to a state of divine importance.

Louis XI was Ludwig's patron saint, and it doesn't take a genius to understand why King Ludwig might have perceived some connection between himself and a Medieval king who was later elevated to sainthood.

However, the ties run deeper than you may initially imagine. King Ludwig arguably believed that he was the reincarnation of a later French ruler - Louis XIV of France. Louis XIV was a direct descendant of Louis XI and Ludwig was related by blood to Louis XIV, too.

There were more tenuous connections - the name Ludwig is the Germanic equivalent of Louis, and Ludwig derived supernatural importance from Louis' famous declaration of "l'etat, c'est moi". Ludwig interpreted it to be a linguistic connection to the nearby town of Ettal - an anagram of the letters from the famous phrase. He therefore chose this auspicious spot to build Linderhof Palace.

The Dressing Room

The oak-walled dressing room is relatively simple, compared to the preceding rooms, but it's the ceiling that has particular interest - there's a wooden trellis over the painted ceiling, aiming to give the impression that the room is open to the sky above.

The murals on the wall idolise the lives of two Medieval poets - Vogelwieide and Sachs.

The Living Room

The Living Room is extensively decorated with the mythology of the Medieval Knight Lohengrin - one of the most important motifs in Ludwig's obsessions. Ludwig saw a deep connection between himself and Lohengrin, the so-called 'swan knight', who aspired to a life of honour and virtue, but was tragically condemned to eternal loneliness.

An entire alcove of the L-shaped room is dedicated to imagery of the swan, including a vast ceramic swan, which was intended as a container for luxuriant flowers.

Grotto

If there was any doubt about Ludwig's eccentricity up to this point, the interior decor of Neuschwanstein takes a truly bizarre turn once you leave the Living Room, and enter the indoor grotto.

Complete with fake rocks, an artificial waterfall (since switched off) and evocative coloured lighting, the grotto wouldn't look out of place in a theme-park. Its significance, rather, was to evoke some of the scenes of Wagner's Tannhäuser, which are continued in the adjacent study.

A glass door in the rocks (not presently visible) would have lead to a Winter Garden - a glass room boasting spectacular Alpine views.

It's said that the waterfall in the grotto was designed as a compromise - Ludwig wanted a cascade of mountain water to crash down a palace staircase, evoking the atmosphere of the Tannhäuser. Some of the castle architects proposed the grotto as a more practical solution to his crazed desire.

Study

The sizeable study is decorated in a neo-Gothic style. Ludwig's writing desk still takes pride of place. The murals around the room depict more scenes from Wager's Tannhäuser, developing the narrative from the preceding grotto.

The Singers' Hall

The upper floor of the castle - the fourth floor - is almost entirely consumed by the Singer's Hall - which was debatably the most

Singer's Hall. Photo taken 1886.

important (and still the most impressive) section of
Neuschwanstein.

The room is modelled on two separate rooms from Wartburg
Castle - the Festival Hall and also the Singer's Hall. The Singer's
Hall was apparently the location of the famous Medieval
minstrel's contest in 1207 (a motif we've seen before in the Dining
Room, and the story which inspired Wagner's Tannhäuser).

Curiously, rather than depict the singing contest within the
murals, Ludwig commissioned a series of paintings which tell the
story of Parzival and the Holy Grail.

The final image - perhaps befittingly - is of Parzival's son,
Lohengrin. Lohengrin was, of course, the swan knight. Including
this painting may have been a conscious decision to try and tie

together all the imagery we've seen previously - all of the three key motifs are brought together in one final scene.

In 1886, Ludwig tragically got wind of the fact that his Parliament had declared him insane, and were imminently to depose him. He had one last night in the castle before he was lead away - and its said that he spend this time pacing the Singer's Room, which had only been finished days before. As he paced, it's said that he desperately recited sections from Wagner's work, knowing it would be the last time he'd set foot inside his magnificent creation.

Up until 2014, a world-renowned series of classical music concerts were held in the Singer's Hall each September. A scaled-down version was held in 2015 and it's not exactly clear if the series will continue into 2016/2017. If you're interested, the best bet is to check in with the Schwangau tourism association: https://www.schwangau.de/aktuelles/.

The End of the Tour - The Kitchen and Knight's Bathhouse

The main tour ends as you exit the Singer's Room and descend into the bowels of the Palas; but it's possible to spend a little time passing through the castle kitchens at your own pace. Evidently, Ludwig would never have had cause to set foot here, so they're much more restrained - although the modern heating system and electricity is of note.

The final descent to the giftshops (note the plural!) is through the bare-brick foundations of the Knight's Bathhouse - intended as a mythical dipping-pool for young knights. Ludwig initially conceived that these rooms would take on a Moorish theme: it was never realised.

King Ludwig II in General's Uniform and Coronation Robe
Ferdinand von Piloty, 1865

3.0 A King and His Castle: The Life of Ludwig II

Rather like Henry VIII or Elizabeth I, the myth and magic of King Ludwig II has permeated the popular imagination.

His ostentatious castles and palaces, eccentric beliefs, and murky personal life have combined to create a powerful mythology.

The unresolved questions around his life - particularly the mystery of his death - have fuelled ongoing conspiracy theories. In fact, the enigma of the king has helped to preserve the public's interest for more than a hundred years - perhaps because speculation and doubt fire the imagination much more than any solved mystery could.

Rather than a chronological discussion of Ludwig's life, I've tried to explain a number of key questions about the monarch, which may help unravel some of the mysteries of Neuschwanstein.

What Was Life Like for Ludwig Whilst Growing Up?

Without delving into pop-psychoanalysis, Ludwig had a somewhat difficult childhood. He was raised by two distant parents, and was always reported to be a loner who preferred his own company.

The boy was a little eccentric from the fore: he detested physical ugliness in anyone, and refused to be waited on - or even to look at - ugly servants.

Writers at the time described Ludwig as having a 'black and white' style of thinking. He considered others to either be perfect or failed, and had idealistic view of human emotions - such as love and friendship. These ideas seemed to be formed from reading fiction, rather than from any interactions with other people.

He was, by all accounts, a handsome and dashing young man, and his appearance was widely praised in contemporary letters. As he grew older, he grew fat and lost his teeth: in an individual previously so obsessed with beauty, this must have had a significant psychological impact.

He was frequently described as a troubled young man who tortured himself for his failings. He saw mistakes as proof that he was a fundamentally flawed individual - rather than just being human. It's very likely that he was gay (see below for more), and this doubtless contributed to his mental turmoil.

His father died unexpectedly, when Ludwig was just 18. He was forced onto the throne with little preparation for rule.

Why Was King Ludwig Obsessed With Medieval Times and the Concept of Absolute Monarchy?

Ludwig's obsession with Medieval times probably began after spending childhood summers in Hohenschwangau Castle. He played the role of a little prince every summer - and this is bound to have stimulated his attraction to the past.

The main reason for his preoccupation with times gone by, however, was contemporary politics. Just two years after he became King, Bavaria was dragged into the Prussian-Austrian war. Ludwig detested battle, and he unfortunately sided with Austria - the losing country.

As a result of his country's loss, Bavaria effectively became an annex of the greater Prussian state. It was a political disaster - Bavaria had previously been an autonomous country, and instead it was subsumed into a much greater political power.

We shouldn't be too hard on Ludwig - politically, the wind was changing, and the growth of Prussia was almost irresistible. Bavaria's loss may have been inevitable. However, as a result, Ludwig's role as monarch was transformed from a reasonably powerful leader to little more than a vassal of Prussia. He became an impotent king.

The defeat, it's said, haunted him through the rest of his life. His obsession with Medieval times - where kings were divinely granted power from God, and reigned unchallenged over their country with the unwavering respect of their subjects - seems to have been a response to his personal lack of power.

What Was The Relationship Between King Ludwig and the Composer Richard Wagner?

I really can't over-emphasize the importance of Richard Wagner to King Ludwig, and of King Ludwig to Wagner. Theirs was a truly synergistic relationship: neither would have achieved artistic greatness without the other.

Ludwig was obsessed with Wagner's opera from an early age. In 1861, he was entranced with productions of the composer's Lohengrin, and the Tannhäuser. One of Ludwig's first actions on assuming the throne in 1864 was to invite Wagner to the palace to discuss his music and artistry.

From there onwards, the men's friendship blossomed: they exchanged more than 600 letters, met routinely, and discussed the artistic emblems and fables which would become so important in Wagner's music, and Ludwig's architecture.

Ludwig's contribution to Wagner's success was partially financial. Ludwig provided Wagner with extremely generous financial patronage of around 1 million marks over his lifetime; alongside with luxury lodgings and some degree of political impunity. This infuriated much of the high society in Munich, as Wagner had a terrible reputation. He was publicly perceived as a disgraced philanderer, continually chased by creditors as a result of previous debts.

In addition to the finances to support Wagner's artistry, Ludwig also assisted the composer with the production of his works. His support facilitated the staging of Tristan and Isolde in the National Theatre in 1865 - a truly unprecedented honour. It was Wagner's first successful production for 15 years.

Indeed, due to the continuing financial support of Ludwig, the previews of Wagner's next three works of the Ring saga - Die Meistersinger von Nürnberg, Das Rheingold and Die Walküre - were also performed in Munich. The city was transformed into one of the cultural hubs of Europe.

To celebrate this fact - and perhaps to immortalise his beloved Wagner - Ludwig planned to create a vast concert hall in central Munich to honour the composer. Financial constraints and political pressures meant that such plans were scaled down as time went on, resulting in the construction of the Festspielhaus Hall in Bayreuth, completed in 1876.

Evidently, Wagner's artistry influenced King Ludwig profoundly. Many of the rooms within Neuschwanstein - most notably the Singer's Hall, Dining Room and Grotto - explicitly depict scenes from Lohengrin and the Tannhäuser, and of the Norse mythology and imagery which inspired these operas.

Fundamentally, Ludwig's construction of Neuschwanstein was intended to be the physical embodiment of the music and ethos of Wagner's operatic works, and the ultimate cumulation of their artistic union was intended to be in the performance of opera within the castle.

What was King Ludwig's Sexuality?

This is one question which has fired imagination over the years, and one question where there can be a pretty definite answer. By modern standards, it's almost certain that Ludwig was gay. Of course, attitudes to homosexuality were quite different during late c19th Germany - and it's easy to suppose that these attitudes contributed to Ludwig's tortured mental state.

Ludwig was never really involved with any woman during his life. In 1867, he was briefly engaged to Sophie, Duchess of Bavaria, but it was a remarkably cold engagement that lasted only nine months. Ludwig appeared appalled at the idea of kissing his fiancee on the lips (he would only kiss her upon her brow) and their public appearances appeared extremely forced - indeed, he swept off from a ball at the Foreign Ministry without even saying goodbye to Sophie.

Ludwig broke off the ill-fated engagement after postponing the marriage twice - a rather unthinkable act of rudeness. He was only pressured into making a decision by his future father-in-law, Duke Max, who was exasperated at his ungentlemany behaviour. Ludwig's eventual letter to Sophie, calling off the whole sorry saga, spoke of a "brotherly love" that was "not the kind of love required for a union".

Instead, Ludwig reportedly suffered numerous infatuations with young men - most infamously young countrymen who he met on horse-rides, and some of his male servants and calvary-men. Some of the subjects of his infatuation included an aide-de-camp

Baron von Varicourt; and another aide, Paul Taxis. The available volumes of Ludwig's private diaries attest to his illicit obsessions.

Ludwig's retinue also organised infamous all-night gatherings exclusively for local young countrymen, which involved drinking, dancing and what was euphemistically termed 'horseplay'. The meetings were subject to endless popular gossip about the King's proclivities.

The stories became even more salacious later within the King's reign when - it was alleged - some of his more unscrupulous advisors began to orchestrate meetings between the King and calvary soldiers, knowing that they could later blackmail the weakened King using their knowledge of his activities.

The situation was so severe that, in 1886, the Council of Ministers took the unprecedented step of writing to the King to expressing deep concern about some of the circulating rumours, and willed him to desist.

Why Did King Ludwig Fall From Power?

It's a common misconception that Ludwig's obsession for building castles bankrupted the Bavarian state. He did, however, drain the fortune of the Royal family, and was starting to accrue significant debts - which, by 1885, consisted of more than 14 million marks.

These liabilities were so significant that the Bavarian government might have had needed to back the loans.

The crux of the problem was that his obsession with castle construction seemed insatiable. Despite frequent warnings - from the highest political levels - that his profligacy needed to stop, Ludwig's obsession continued unabated. When the Bavarian state refused to lend him any more money, he instead tried to reach out to foreign governments for loans - rather like an addict desperate for a fix.

In addition to his intemperate spending, the King had become absolutely disinterested in the business of State. He would frequently neglect his political duties and postpone important decisions, instead choosing to obsess over tiny details of his architectural work.

Essentially, Ludwig quickly becoming a financial and political headache for the Parliament of Bavaria. However, it was nigh-on impossible to depose him through constitutional means.

There was one loophole: a monarch could be forced to abdicate on grounds of ill-health. Despite no previous diagnosis of mental illness, in 1886, Parliament obtained the professional opinions of four separate psychiatrists, who all assessed the patient to not be of sane mind.

It's worth pointing out that none of the psychiatrists formally assessed Ludwig in person.

In June 1886, a party travelled to meet and section Ludwig - passing the throne of Bavaria to Prince Regent Luitpold.

Was King Ludwig Really Mad?

There are certain factors that would predispose Ludwig to mental illness. We know that some mental illnesses have a genetic link, and Ludwig's brother, Otto, was entirely incapacitated by psychotic thoughts. In the early 1870s, Otto stopped eating or sleeping; he began to hear voices; and started acting inappropriately (for example, barking like a dog).

In 1878, Otto was declared insane. He was held (effectively as a prisoner) in one of the royal castles. His mental state worsened still further over time, and he began to lose his memory. In the end, Otto outlived Ludwig (Otto died in 1916), but, due to his insanity, the Bavarian throne passed to Prince Luitpold after Ludwig died.

Ludwig himself reportedly suffered from hallucinations. For example, aged 13, it was recorded that he heard voices in other rooms of the palace.

However, Ludwig's most severe symptoms were delusional beliefs, detached from everyday reality. From the early years, Ludwig had always been a dreamer, but certain traits and characteristics suggest an unhealthy attachment to fantasy. He repeatedly signed letters not from himself but from fictional characters with whom he identified (most often the good knight, Parzival); and dressed up as characters from Wagner's operas - assuming their entire identity.

Ludwig's last years in power represented a descent into total detachment from everyday reality. His fantasy and extravagance knew no bounds: infamously, he sent an envoy around the world to try and find land for a new kingdom. In addition to this wild profligacy, he entirely ignored all threats of bankruptcy, ploughing more money into building castles, despite frequent warnings that he was entirely penniless.

More comically, he began to fly into rages and tantrums with his servants - rather like the Queen of Hearts, he began to threaten staff with beheadings or deportation for any who disobeyed him. He also invited his favourite grey horse to dinner - during which time she inevitably smashed the crockery - and attempted to send an aide to Italy in order to recruit a number of robbers, whom he could bribe to depose the despised Prussian Crown Prince.

In his final days, on hearing that he was to be deposed, he tried to mount a counter-coup, proposing to that his barber should lead his political cabinet.

Besides such comical delusions, there were more sinister features to his mood. During his final years, the king effectively became nocturnal - sleeping in the day and riding aimlessly at night. He became a loner - eating, dining and living alone - and became obsessed with poison, and the idea of suicide.

When he was deposed from the throne, the sectioning psychiatrist diagnosed a form of insanity and psychosis which would correspond with the modern day diagnosis of schizophrenia.

Of course, it's hard to distinguish if the diagnosis was correct - or a convenient way to shift an extravagant and increasingly disgraced monarch from office.

How Did King Ludwig Die?

We know that Ludwig died on June 13, 1886. His corpse was found floating in Lake Starnberg - alongside the body of his psychiatrist, Dr Gudden. The rest, really, remains a mystery.

Ludwig had been removed from power (and from beloved Neuschwanstein) two days' prior, and had been taken to Berg Castle, alongside his psychiatrist and a team of carers.

It's said that the patient was doing well, and his psychiatrist was content to join him on a walk around the nearby lake.

We don't know what happened next. Various theories abound – that one murdered the other and the other party died in the struggle; than an unknown assassin murdered both; or that the deaths were a freak accident - perhaps as the result of Ludwig attempting to escape, or commit suicide.

The verdict is very much open, but different groups of King Ludwig aficionados have pointed to differing shreds of evidence to further their interpretation of the mystery.

My own reading is that any kind of murder would have been unlikely - there's no record whatsoever of Ludwig ever acting violently, and a psychiatrist (that's supposing he had a motive) would have had neater solutions to bump off a patient - solutions which wouldn't have put him in such physical danger. I'd attribute the happenings to accident or to misadventure; but this is very much conjecture.

As there are no firm answers to the riddle, the interested can definitely fire up Google and find a vast array of conspiracy theories to tempt the imagination.

3.1 Exploring King Ludwig's Other Castles

Neuschwanstein isn't the only of King Ludwig's creations, and it needs to be appreciated in the context of the king's other castles. These are Hohenschwangau Castle; Linderhof Palace; and Herrenchimsee Palace. Hohenschwangau is, of course, detailed below.

As the crow flies, **Linderhof Palace** is only about 30km from Neuschwanstein, and is tucked into a gorgeous hollow between towering Alpine mountains. Unfortunately, its remote location makes it a headache to reach, and it takes a few hours circular drive through the Alps to actually access the palace and park.

Linderhof is actually quite small - effectively a summer-house which Ludwig converted into a spectacular little palace. It's the only one of his creations which he actually finished, and he spent more time here during his adult life than in anywhere else.

As you approach, the marble-white exterior of Linderhof actually looks quite restrained: it's only on entering do you get a sense of the king's overwhelming eccentricity.

Linderhof Palace.

The prevailing sentiment within the interior design brief appears to have been 'one can never have too much gold leaf', and virtually every luxuriant room is coated in the stuff - a riot of decadence that borders on claustrophobic. Indeed, the one passageway coated in silver-leaf seems like a welcome relief.

The palace gardens are particularly interesting, as they contain a scattering of eccentrically themed summer houses, including a little Moorish sitting-room. The star of the attraction though is the Grotto.

This little den was a haven of artifice - a man-made cave equipped with a wave-machine and state-of-the-art electric lights. It was intended to evoke one of the first scenes of Wagner's Tannhäuser, but, to me, it almost looks like Ludwig sought to create a Disneyworld-esque experience years ahead of its time.

The other of Ludwig's four residences, **Herrenchiemsee Palace**, is quite different to the other three sites - and is consequently least visited by tourists.

Rather than an Alpine retreat, Herrenchiemsee is located in the flat, rolling farmlands to the East of Munich. The Chiemsee is a vast inland lake ('The Bavarian Sea'), and the palace is perched on the picturesque Herreninsel island within the lake. You'll resultantly need to hop on a boat trip to get there.

Herrenchiemsee raises eyebrows because of the brazen eccentricity behind Ludwig's vision: the palace was to intended to emulate and better the design of Versailles in France. Ludwig idolised King Louis XIV (to the extent of convincing himself that he was Louis' re-incarnation - the name Ludwig, of course, is the German equivalent to Louis). Resultantly, he sought to rebuild Versailles on German soil.

As follies go, nothing really rivals Herrenchiemsee, but there's a certain interest in seeing the place. It was very far from being completed at Ludwig's death (and in some senses, was never intended to be complete - many of the rooms were designed to always remain empty - there only to give the palace scale).

Some sections of the palace even exceed Versailles - the famed Hall of Mirrors is actually longer than its original counterpart, although the decor is remarkably faithful.

What King Ludwig's Castles Have in Common: And How They Compare to Neuschwanstein

Despite the fact that we'd think of some of King Ludwig's creations as being palaces rather than castles (the German word 'schloss' is interchangeable), there're strong unifying elements which run through the design and planning of all these spots.

All of the castles are (ironically enough, having been built for a recluse) designed to externally impress. Basically, every one has been engineered to create a 'wow' when you first see it.

For example, the Marienbrücke bridge, at Neuschwanstein, was re-engineered to provide a phenomenal view of the castle - and the same can be said of the grand approach to Herrenchimsee - designed to be an entrance via horse and cart through impressive gardens and tree-lined boulevards.

The next unifying factor - which is quite closely linked to the first - is that the design of all these spots is quite obviously theatrical. This shouldn't necessarily surprise - stage-designers were involved with the layout of every single one of these palaces - but all the buildings possess a certain self-consciousness, having been designed to evoke certain feelings in an an observer.

It's also important to appreciate that each of the buildings is exquisitely tailored to the landscape around it. This can't be emphasised enough. King Ludwig agonised over the surroundings for each of his castles, and the architecture of each perfectly compliments the natural environment around.

For example, Neuschwanstein soars upwards, and its sharper lines and more defined turrets compliment the sharp angles and tall peaks of the Alpine rock-faces alongside. By contrast, Herrenchiemsee has horizontal length rather than vertical height - complimenting perfectly the flat plains of its home island.

This interplay between environment and architecture is something remarkable, and makes King Ludwig's creations stand out for observers who are otherwise a bit sniffy about his overblown style.

3.2 Disney and Neuschwanstein: The Connection Between The Castles

Many visitors know Neuschwanstein Castle as the 'Disney Castle' - the inspiration behind the castles in the Disney themeparks in California and Florida.

If you visit either themepark, you can see elements of Neuschwanstein in Sleeping Beauty's Castle (the first Disney castle to be built, in Anaheim, CA) and also in Cinderella's Castle (Walt Disney World, FL). However, these castles weren't based on Neuschwanstein alone.

Disney's designers - the imagineers - actually toured Europe to find inspiration for Disneyland's Fantasyland. The inspiration for both their castle creations came from a variety of sources. These

This iconic photograph of Neuschwanstein Castle - taken in the 1890s - made the castle internationally famous.

included numerous French chateaux - including Fontainebleu, Pierrefonds, Chambord and Chaudmont. I've heard that they also visited the Alcazar of Segovia, in Spain - personally one of my favourite castles in Europe, but I suspect that this might well be an urban myth, as I can't find any evidence of that trip.

It's definitely an urban myth that Walt Disney ever visited Neuschwanstein - he sent a team of designers to do his bidding. It's likewise entirely false that Walt intervened in Allied air-raids during WWII, forbidding them from bombing Neuschwanstein.

Evidently, Walt wouldn't have had much say in matters of international conflict, and, in any case, there were pre-existing agreements between the Allies and Germany upon the preservation of cultural sites. Additionally, Neuschwanstein had no strategic significance for military endeavour.

So, which architectural elements of the Disney castles were 'borrowed' from Neuschwanstein? Do remember that Neuschwanstein itself probably 'borrowed' architectural elements from the French castles I've mentioned, which were built long before it!

However, in Disney's Cinderella's Castle in Walt Disney World, it's the two tall towers with witches-hat turrets which bear quite a resemblance to Neuschwanstein. The lighter-brick gatehouse, which contrasts to the smoother finish of the upper castle, also looks quite Neuschwanstein-y to me - alongside some of the embossed bower designs, halfway up the castle's taller towers.

Neuschwanstein and the Disney castles share more than just architecture, of course. All three castles were purposefully designed to capture the essence of a fairytale fortress in bricks and mortar. And, what's more, each castle was designed to create a powerful, emotional reaction in any visitor to the place. So, I guess, you could say that Uncle Walt continued with the projects which King Ludwig started.

Shutterstock /Danshutter

3.3 Slipping Away: Erosion and Neuschwanstein

As an aside, it's worth mentioning that Neuschwanstein causes more than its fair share of headaches for its managing authority: the Bavarian Palaces Department.

Evidently, the castle was designed to accommodate one reclusive king: it was never envisaged to become the biggest tourist attraction in Germany (and one of the foremost in Western Europe).

The sheer numbers of visitors, in conjunction with its precarious position and the harsh alpine winters, means that it requires a phenomenal amount of care to just preserve Neuschwanstein.

The rocky outcrop is notoriously unstable, and vulnerable to erosion. In recent years, the Bavarian Palace Authority have been forced to drill deeper steel foundations into the bedrock to combat the subsidence facing some sections of the castle.

In addition, the external white limestone cladding, although beautiful, is extremely vulnerable to the snow and ice. As recently as three years ago, two entire frontages of the castle had to be re-clad to keep up appearances.

In the last 18 months, efforts have turned to the Marienbrücke bridge, which was literally creaking beneath the number of tourists. Once this is done, it's on to the next project. It's not inconceivable that, in the not-too-distant future, access to the castle might need to be even more strictly limited to preserve the place for future generations.

3.4 Neuschwanstein and King Ludwig: A Timeline

1832 - Ludwig's father, Maximilian, refurbishes Hohenschwangau Castle (opposite modern-day Neuschwanstein) in a mock-Medieval style. Prince Ludwig would spend his future summers here.

25 August, 1845 - Ludwig is born in Nymphenburg Palace, Munich.

1850 - Ludwig's father builds the Marienbrücke Bridge, out of wood (it was rebuilt in iron in 1866). It's now a spectacular viewpoint for looking onto Neuschwanstein Castle.

1850s - Ludwig spends many of his summers in the Alpine valley of Hohenschwangau Village. He would often visit the site of the modern day Neuschwanstein Castle, where there lay the remains of two older castles (Vorder Castle and Hinterhohenschwangau).

10 March, 1864 - Ludwig's father dies unexpectedly. Ludwig becomes King of Bavaria.

4 May, 1864 - One of Ludwig's first acts in power is to summon Wagner to his court.

1866 - Austro-Prussian war. Bavaria sides with Austria - and loses. The defeat of Bavaria means that the country effectively becomes an annex of Prussia - and King Ludwig loses control of his armies. It's a disaster for Bavaria, rendering Ludwig - and future kings - relatively impotent.

Early 1868 - Ludwig begins to commission the first plans for Neuschwanstein Castle.

Summer 1868 - Preparation of the foundations of Neuschwanstein begin.

5 September, 1869 - The foundation stone of Neuschwanstein Castle is laid.

1870/71 - Franco-Prussian war. The King's allegiance now falls with Prussia.

1872 - Neuschwanstein Gatehouse completed. As of 1873, Ludwig used the upper rooms of the Gatehouse as his accommodation when visiting the building site.

1880 - Main outer buildings of the residential section of the castle ('The Palas') completed.

10 June, 1886 - Ludwig declared not of sound mind, and unfit for office. Prince Luitpold assumes the royal title.

12 June, 1886 - Ludwig is transferred to Berg Castle, intended as a secure prison.

13 June, 1886 - King Ludwig dies in mysterious circumstances, alongside his psychiatrist, in Lake Starnberg.

1892 - Building work within Neuschwanstein ceases. The Bower and the Square Tower are completed, but to a much smaller scale than originally planned.

4.0 The Practicalities: Planning And Organising Your Visit

4.1 Ten Tips To Make the Most of Your Trip to Neuschwanstein

Statue in the snow

Keen to maximise your visit? Here're my top tips to eke the most out of your trip - whilst minimising the inconvenience of the huge crowds.

Tip 1: Visit the Marienbrücke iron bridge for a spectacular view

The one must-do of any visit to Neuschwanstein is to take in the view from the Marienbrücke iron bridge. The bridge is about a 15 minute walk from Neuschwanstein, and the views are absolutely spell-binding. If you're looking for the ultimate trip photo, this is the place to come.

Indeed, if you're a keen photographer, my advice is to visit the bridge in the late afternoon. The light will be at its best as the sun fades towards the end of the day, and the shadows will accentuate the outcrop beneath Neuschwanstein.

It's also worth mentioning that, elsewhere in the world, the Marienbrücke might be an attraction in itself. It arches gently over a dramatic, 80-metre gorge - just looking down is a kind of impressive experience. However, here, such trivialities are rather overshadowed by Neuschwanstein!

More about the Marienbrücke view is on p61.

Note that the Marienbrücke was closed for much of the 2015 season for structural work. It should be open as normal from May 2016.

Tip 2: Visit in the spring or autumn

Not everyone's going to be able to achieve this, I realise, but you will have a different experience of the castle if you can visit in a slightly milder climate, and when there are fewer other visitors.

In the height of summer, Neuschwanstein is extremely busy and the heat can occasionally make some of the surrounding trails and pathways wearing.

Conversely, although the castle may look pretty mid-winter when it's blanketed with snow, it can be bitingly cold, and some of the associated services around will shut. For example, buses to the castle won't be running, and the path to the Marnenbrücke will be closed.

More distressingly, however, is the thick Alpine fog that often descends on winter days: ruining any view you might have had.

Tip 3: Get there as early as you possibly can

Nothing else will transform your experience of Neuschwanstein as much as getting there before the vast crowds of visitors do. Particularly in the summer, the castle is absolutely mobbed - you'll encounter queues for hours just to buy tickets, and the place can sometimes sell-out.

The only way to see the inside of the castle is via a guided tour, and, as the day wears on, groups include vast numbers (of usually noisy students) who will be ushered quickly around the rooms, with little time to explain or really appreciate the details of the castle.

Resultantly, do all you can to get to the castle early - as soon as it opens, if at all possible, in the summer (generally 9am). At this time of day, the crowds are lighter and the tour guides are fresher - you're likely to enjoy a better tour experience when the guides are starting out on a sunny morning, rather than after four hours of shouting over noisy students.

Getting there early can present problems, so see my next tip on how to achieve it.

Tip 4: Stay as close as you can afford, for at least one night

If you're able to stay one or more nights near Neuschwanstein, do so. Many people visit Neuschwanstein as a day trip from Munich - the most common hopping-off point for international flights. This is OK, but bear in mind that you'll be travelling for around 2.5hrs in each direction, so you're not going to be able to get there early.

If you choose to stay in Hohenschwangau Village, there's nothing more impressive than waking up early and looking out of your hotel window to see Neuschwanstein appearing through the mist. It's predictably a bit costly, but it's not out-of-the-way expensive: and it'll transform your experience, as it makes it so easy to reach the castle early.

Tip 5: Beg or plead with your ticket times

There are three attractions worth seeing in Hohenschwangau Village - Neuschwanstein Castle itself, Hohenschwangau Castle (where Ludwig spent time as a prince - effectively Neuschwanstein's sister castle), and a new Museum of Bavarian Kings.

You can wander into the Museum of Bavarian Kings whenever you wish, but the entry to the insides of Neuschwanstein and Hohenschwangau Castle is strictly via a timed tour.

You can buy a combination ticket to both Neuschwanstein and Hohenschwangau Castle, which'll save you a bit of money. However, annoyingly, the management agency which deals with ticketing decrees that if you buy a combo saver ticket to both Neuschwanstein and Hohenschwangau, your first tour will be of Hohenschwangau Castle - and you'll get a later time for Neuschwanstein.

It's an annoying rule, as there's no pressing urgency to reach Hohenschwangau Castle early (it receives one million fewer visitors a year than its sibling); whereas an early tour to Neuschwanstein is pretty much a pre-requisite.

You can either try and bargain with the vendor at the ticket booth (which is very seldom successful: this is not a country where you can bend the rules) or you can suck up the extra cost and just buy two separate tickets if you wish to see both. This is definitely the best option.

Tip 6: Make the most of the Alpine environment - hit the trails or row a boat

Neuschwanstein is set in a beautiful Alpine environment, and if you're an outdoorsy soul, it'd be a shame not to experience some of the surroundings.

There's a small network of hiking trails in the area around the castle - notably one up the Tegelberg Mountain, which affords spectacular views back onto Neuschwanstein. Alternatively, in

Summer, you can hire a small rowing boat and strike out onto one of the two adjacent Alpine lakes - the Alpsee and the Schwansee. See my section on Hohenschwangau for more (p93).

Tip 7: Ride a horse and cart

If you're a true romantic at heart, then you should definitely choose to ride up to Neuschwanstein's entrance by horse and cart.

Of course, there are various different ways to reach the castle from the village below (you could walk uphill for 40 minutes, or take a tourist shuttle bus) but there's some romance about reaching the castle exactly as King Ludwig would have.

Tip 8: Explore Hohenschwangau Castle & the Museum of Bavarian Kings

If you've come all this way to see Neuschwanstein Castle, it'd be frankly remiss to skip over two beautiful attractions in Hohenschwangau Village: neighbouring custard-yellow Hohenschwangau Castle (a summer holiday home for young Ludwig) and the adjacent, newly constructed, Museum of Bavarian Kings.

Both help provide context on Neuschwanstein: and help you to understand why King Ludwig was driven to build the place. See p94 for more.

Tip 9: Get to know more about King Ludwig II

For me, the castles come alive if you can understand a bit more about the feverish imagination of King Ludwig. A lot of architecture buffs baulk at Neuschwanstein - certain parts definitely border on kitsch - but an appreciation for the true eccentric drive of the king, and of the images and mythology that occupied him, will help you appreciate a lot of the detail of his work.

Tip 10: Split your visit over two half days

I've included an entire 'ideal itinerary' for trips to Neuschwanstein Castle. It's on p63.

4.2 Touring Options

Broadly speaking, there are three possible touring-plans for any visit to Neuschwanstein.

A little 101 on German geography will help you get your bearings, and some idea of which plan might be the best for you.

Neuschwanstein Castle lies on the high side of an Alpine valley, overlooking the village of Hohenschwangau below. It's a short walk between village and castle.

The nearest town is Medieval Füssen, which is about 15min by bus from the village.

The most logical adjacent big city is Munich, which is around 130km (80 miles) from the castle. All these three places - the village, the town and the city - a worth a visit in their own right.

Option 1: Staying in Munich, and Visiting Neuschwanstein As A Day-Trip

The majority of visitors to Neuschwanstein stay in Munich and visit the castle as a day-trip - for better or worse.

This option entails about a two-hour train ride from Munich, followed by a 15min bus ride each way.

You can alternatively join an organised tour (a recommended route) or drive yourself (be warned that parking can be a headache). For both these options, expect about a 2hr drive in each direction.

For more on staying in Munich and visiting Neuschwanstein as a day-trip, have a look at my section on Munich (p75).

Option 2: Staying Closer to Neuschwanstein In The Town of Füssen

The next option is to stay in Füssen for a night or two. Füssen is around 10km from Hohenschwangau Village.

Virtually everyone who visits Neuschwanstein Castle from Munich needs to pass through Füssen anyway, so you're effectively just breaking a journey. Here, you'd enjoy the luxury of lodging much closer to the castles - it's only a 15 minute bus trip.

Füssen has more in terms of lodgings and night-life than Hohenschwangau village, and it's proportionally a bit cheaper too.

For more on staying in Füssen and visiting Neuschwanstein, have a look at p84.

Option 3: (Recommended) - Staying At the Foot of Neuschwanstein in Hohenschwangau Village

The third option is to stay directly in Hohenschwangau. There's nothing comparable to waking up in the morning and gazing up at Neuschwanstein, before the thousands (and, in the summer, tens of thousands) of other tourists arrive.

If you have the time, it's definitely my recommended option. More on p93.

As a foot-note, you might be a born optimist and planning on visiting the castle from some city further away - say Stuttgart or Innsbruck.

Visiting Neuschwanstein From Innsbruck

Some tourists visit Neuschwanstein from Innsbruck in Austria, and although it's not impossible, it's more of a headache. The best option is to drive the 125km to the castles, although parking is going to be a frustration.

If you want to take public transport, you can take a train from Innsbruck to Reutte, a town on the Austrian border that's around 20km from Füssen. You'll almost certainly need to change trains in Garmisch-Partenkirchen and the journey this far will be 2h40min or so.

From Reutte, it's a 20min drive to Füssen. There are local buses which take around 25min to Füssen, but they're irregular and you may wish instead to take a taxi (around €30). From Füssen, just take the regular buses to the castles (as per the Füssen section in the main guide).

(An alternative option to cut down the taxi fare is to take another train connection from Reutte to Vils, a small village which is only 10min from Füssen. The taxi then will only be about €15 - but this route is a real pain, and only saves a little bit of money).

Transport from Innsbruck to Reutte can be checked using www.oebb.at/en/

Transport from Reutte to Füssen can be be searched via Deutsche Bahn, www.bahn.com. Note that you need to input 'Reutte in Tirol' to get the right station.

Visiting Neuschwanstein From Stuttgart

It is possible to visit Neuschwanstein as a day-trip from Stuttgart, but you're in for a monster day. High speed trains link Stuttgart to Augsburg, where you'll change onto a regional connection to Füssen.

This journey is about 3h40min each leg. You'll then need to catch the bus from Füssen to the castle (see the Füssen section, below).

Research transport from Stuttgart to Füssen using Deutsche Bahn, www.bahn.com.

4.3 The Essentials of Neuschwanstein: Tickets, Timings and Tours

Neuschwanstein Entrance Ticket

Neuschwanstein Castle overlooks Hohenschwangau Village - and Hohenschwangau acts as your access point to the castle, with all the facilities you might need - including a small array of restaurants, hotels, and shops. The village is also home to two other attractions - Hohenschwangau Castle and the Museum of the Bavarian Kings.

Opening Dates & Times

Neuschwanstein Castle is open to tourists pretty much every day of the year. It's closed only on Dec 24, 25th, 31st, and January 1st.

Summer opening hours (between March 19 and October 15 2016) are every day from 9am until 6pm. Winter hours (from October 16 2016 - March 18 2017) are every day from 10am until 4pm. For completenesses' sake, note that Hohenschwangau Castle only closes on December 24th. Its opening times are near enough as per Neuschwanstein.

Weather and When to Visit

Neuschwanstein is an Alpine destination. From October to early April, you should expect some snow. It can be very cold, so bring warm clothes and decent boots. Be aware that, although the village is used to coping with blizzards, some attractions may be closed on very snowy days (the buses don't run, for example, and in windy conditions the Marienbrücke viewing bridge may be closed).

Thick snowfall will also make visibility (and photographs) disappointing.

Summer temperatures are seldom overbearing, although, in combination with the crowds, it can get quite hot indeed in July and August. Bring a hat and suncream.

If you'd like to check out the weather today, the local tourist organisation has a webcam. See https://www.schwangau.de/aktuelles/

Buying Tickets (DON'T make this mistake!)

Don't trek up to the castle expecting to buy a ticket at the gates. You absolutely cannot get one there (so many tourists make that mistake every year) - don't even try!

The Ticketing Centre in Hohenschwangau village is the only official ticketing stop for either purchasing on the day or picking up pre-booked tickets.

In the peak times of summer, there can sometimes be queues of more than 90 minutes to buy tickets - the worst wait tends to occur around lunchtime. On some high season days, tickets also sell out. For that reason, I highly recommend that you book tickets in advance. The web address is https://www.hohenschwangau.de/543.html.

Somewhat cruelly, there's a booking fee of €1.80 per person and per castle (ie, if you book for both castles, that's €3.60). You can cancel a booking with no penalty, up to two hours before your scheduled tour. You can book up to 3pm two days prior. You must collect tickets in person from the ticket centre a minimum of 1hr before your assigned tour (there may still be a bit of a wait, but it won't be a long one). Note that you can only indicate a preferred tour time.

There are a selection of combination tickets which could save a couple of Euros if you wish to visit more than one attraction in Hohenschwangau Village.

2016/7 Prices

Neuschwanstein Ticket Only

Adults - €12
Groups and Students/Seniors - €11
Children under 18 - free

Neuschwanstein & Hohenschwangau Castle Combined

Adults - €23
Groups and Students/Seniors - € 21
Children under 18 - free
Net saving of €1 from the deal

Neuschwanstein, Hohenschwangau Castle & Museum of Bavarian Kings Combined

Adults - €29.50
Groups and Students/Seniors - €28
Children under 18 - free
Net saving of €4 from the deal

As described above, one of the difficulties with these deals is they force you to visit Hohenschwangau Castle first - you therefore hit Neuschwanstein Castle when it's crammed with tourists.

For this reason, I'd actually recommend you skip the minuscule discount and just buy tickets separately if you wish to visit both castles. Make sure your tour for Neuschwanstein is as early as possible.

A development in recent years is that tour operators in Munich are buying up tickets in bulk and reselling them to the public, at a mark-up, advertising the opportunity to 'skip the queue'. There's no harm in using their services, but be aware that you're paying more than face value, and there's also less choice of tour-times.

Tours and Tour Times

The next important point is that you can't walk around Neuschwanstein under your own steam - all visitors must visit as part of a guided tour. (This is mainly for the benefit of the castle management - it's quicker to shepherd tourists through the rooms this way).

Resultantly, you'll be given a specific tour time when you buy your ticket. Tours are conducted in English, German, or with an audioguide.

The tours can often be quite poor (see my section below on 'the perfect itinerary' to try and get the best experience you can) - all I can really recommend otherwise is get there early, as tour-guides tend to be a bit less rushed and a bit more expansive at the start of the day.

Getting to Neuschwanstein Castle from Hohenschwangau Village

Hohenschwangau Village and the Alps. Shutterstock / Lukasz Miegoc

Hohenschwangau Village is in the midst of a valley, and the two castles (that's Hohenschwangau as well as Neuschwanstein) lie on the eastern and western slopes.

Once you've purchased your ticket, do note that you're going to have to scale a bit of an incline to reach either castle. Hohenschwangau is a little walk, but Neuschwanstein is quite a pull up a fairly steep slope. You'll need to have OK mobility and fitness to walk it. Luckily, there are other transport options available.

If you're keen to walk it, the official line is that Neuschwanstein is a 45min walk from the village (and Hohenschwangau Castle takes 30min). The estimate for Neuschwanstein is fair, but most people should be able to manage the walk to Hohenschwangau in something like 20min.

If you don't want to walk it, you have the option of taking a bus, or much more romantically, a horse-drawn carriage, to either castle. These services are charged extra - it's about €6 to go up to the castle by horse (and €3 for the downhill trip); compared to €1.80 upwards (€2.60 return) by bus.

The buses/horses only take around 10-15 minutes to reach Neuschwanstein, but their timetables are surprisingly fluid (surprising for Germany, at least): essentially, they go when they've got enough passengers to go.

If it's snowing, the bus won't run (although the horse-drawn carriages will, unless the conditions are really bad). Bear this in mind if you're visiting in mid-winter.

Neither the bus or the horse-drawn carriages drop you directly at Neuschwanstein - this is because the final approach to the castle is too steep for transport. The horse-drawn carriages drop passengers off below the castle gatehouse, and it's about a 10 minute walk up past a couple of gift-shops and a view-point to reach the castle itself.

The buses curiously drop off passengers above the castle, at the Marienbrücke bridge viewing platform. You can proceed to this viewpoint and then walk down to the castle. This walk is again about 10min, but the viewpoint is spectacular and you'll want to pose for lots of pictures.

Because it takes a little while to reach either castle, you really do need to plan your timings carefully. If you should be late to your tour time, don't expect a shred of empathy for your tardiness - you've missed your tour and you'll have to buy another ticket. This is Germany and such inefficiency goes punished - don't say you haven't been warned.

What To Expect From The Guided Tour

The tour guides you around eleven rooms of Neuschwanstein at a rather breathless pace. It takes about 30min total, of which around 25 minutes are spend in the actual rooms of the castle.

The tour usually consists of 30–50 other visitors, and one harrassed guide. You can either tour in English, German, or they'll give an audioguide to visitors with more exotic languages.

Disappointingly, taking internal photos of the castle is strictly prohibited.

The tour itself is rather whistle-stop - most interested visitors find it isn't enough time - and at the end you'll be thrown out via no less than three different gift-shops (something even DisneyWorld could learn from).

If you join a guided day-trip from Munich, you may have the benefit of the Neuschwanstein tour being done by the guide on your trip - who's usually a bit better than the resident guides, and will be with you for the rest of the day if you've any other questions. Check before booking a tour if this is the case.

(You could book a private tour of the castle for yourself and a group of friends, or a big family. It's predictably expensive and only available in certain hours - see the official website for more. You will need to apply in advance, and will need a group of at least 10).

My guide to each of the rooms of the castle is within the Contexts section.

What To See After Neuschwanstein: The Marienbrücke Viewing Bridge

The Marienbrücke Bridge offers an unmissable perspective of Neuschwanstein Castle and - if you visit when it's open - it's likely to be the highlight of your trip (providing, of course, you're not super-scared of heights....!).

This formidable structure - 'Queen Mary's Bridge' - was built in 1850 by King Ludwig's father, Maximilian, for his consort Mary. Both were keen mountain-climbers: and the bridge was designed in part as a crossing over the dramatic Pöllat gorge, and in part as a viewpoint across the valley. The edifice was originally rendered in wood, but, under the direction of King Ludwig, was rebuilt in 1866 in delicately-cantilevered iron.

Today, standing upon the bridge, you'll enjoy the 'classic view' that you'll have seen in so many promotional photographs: a panorama of Neuschwanstein upon its rocky plinth, with the surrounding lakes and jagged Alps as a backdrop. It's a breathtaking sight.

If you were coming to Neuschwanstein by transit-bus, you'll have been dropped off at the Marienbrücke anyway, but for everyone else, it's about a 15 minute uphill walk from the entrance gatehouse of Neuschwanstein. It's very clearly signposted.

So you're not rushed for time, you might wish to visit the Marienbrücke after going inside Neuschwanstein: that way, you can spend all the time you wish, rather than having to hurry off to your timed tour.

Wintry conditions mean - for safety's sake - that the Marienbrücke isn't open year-round - it's closed when the weather's poor, typically from early October to late March. A surprisingly high number of winter-time visitors choose to vault the guard-rails and pay a visit to the bridge anyway. It's closed for good reason (it's a slippery iron bridge over a vast precipice): avoid the temptation!

As an additional note, structural work means that the Marienbrücke will be closed until May 2016: meaning it's hopefully re-opened by the time you're reading this.

If you're keen on hiking, trails continue on from the other side of the Marienbrücke. See p99.

As a brief aside - whilst we're on the subject of viewing points - there's another outlook of Neuschwanstein located just below the castle gatehouse, approximately where the horse and cart tours drop off visitors. The viewpoint is nowhere near as impressive as the Marienbrücke, but it's worth a look.

Wood-burning stove in restaurant, Füssen

4.4 The Perfect Tour of Neuschwanstein: My Recommended Itinerary

If you're looking for a touring plan to really get the most out of your visit to Neuschwanstein, this is the plan that I'd advise you to take.

- My first piece of advice is that you should stay in Hohenschwangau Village if at all possible (ideally in the Hotel Müller), and aim to arrive around midday on day one.

- Visit Hohenschwangau Castle that afternoon, and perhaps the Museum of Bavarian Kings afterwards, if you have the time. Book your ticket for the first available tour of Neuschwanstein the next day.

- Relax in the evening in your hotel - you could enjoy a meal in Hohenschwangau Village's best restaurant, the Alpenrosen Am See.

- The next morning, get up bright and early and enjoy the vista of Neuschwanstein from your hotel. Travel to the castle to arrive for the very first tour time. Afterwards, proceed to the Marienbrücke and take some photos.

- From there, you could either return to the hotel, collect your luggage and proceed to your next destination, or you could spend some time walking or hiking in the area around Hohenschwangau Village. Or go to the Museum of Bavarian Kings, if you haven't already.

- More on the hotel, the restaurant and the walks is within my section on Hohenschwangau Village.

4.5 Visiting as a Family

Neuschwanstein is a family-friendly destination, and the only problems you're likely to encounter relate to the steep ascent to Neuschwanstein Castle.

The ascent is tricky-to difficult with a stroller (impossible in the winter) and it's likely that you'll need to ride the bus. Note that, on snowy days, buses do not run. Also note that the buses run to the Marienbrücke bridge rather than the castle entrance: you'll still need to walk downhill for around 10-15min to the castle gatehouse.

All the restaurants serve kid-friendly meals and it's easy to pick up basics (for example, suncream) if you've run out. There are changing facilities if you need them.

The internals of the castle might be a bit boring for kids: especially with the time queueing for tours to start. If you're keen to take the tour, bring games and snacks to entertain during the wait.

4.6 Visiting with Reduced Mobility

Visiting with reduced mobility is tricky, but not impossible. You'll need to contact the castle management in advance to book a guided tour which will take into account the one disabled lift within the castle (otherwise, there's lots of stairs).

Getting to Neuschwanstein itself may be tricky. Buses aren't equipped for wheelchair access. You'll need to take a horse and cart, but will need to be able to transfer into this.

The management authorities note that there is one disabled toilet close to the castle.

Horse and cart ride to the castle.

5.0 Saving Money On Your Trip to Neuschwanstein

5.1 Five Money Saving Strategies for a Trip to Neuschwanstein

As an international tourist attraction, visiting Neuschwanstein is a predictably expensive experience, and I'd come prepared for high prices. Having said that, there are ways to save - although the experience is never really going to be cheap.

Tip 1: Using public transport? Pick up a Bayern Ticket

Train travel in Germany can mount up very quickly, and the best way to avoid substantial fares is to pick up a promotional ticket. The Bayern Ticket (Bavarian Ticket) is excellent value, and allows you and up to four others unlimited local travel in Bavaria. It costs €23 a day for the first person, and then €5 for each additional person - huge savings, and it's not widely known about.

If you're planning on visiting Neuschwanstein as a daytrip from Munich with your family, this ticket alone could save you a hundred euros or more. See the section 'saving on on rail travel' just below.

Tip 2: Get a FüssenCard

If you're staying in the town of Füssen, you may be given a FüssenCard (it's technically included in the city tax on each night's stay). If you don't get a card, don't panic - ask nicely at your hotel, and if that doesn't work, pop into the large Tourist Info centre in town and try asking nicely there.

The FussenCard is one money saving strategy for tourists visiting Neuschwanstein.

The main benefit of the card is that it grants you free travel on local buses: including the buses to the castle, which are approximately €2.10 each way. The card also advertises discounts across all attractions around Füssen: in reality, the discounts aren't particularly generous, but it will lop €2 off the ticket price to Neuschwanstein itself. You'll also be able to access public Wifi, as well as an assortment of other (trivial) benefits within the town.

The FüssenCard is electronic and may need to be 'activated' by the hotel owner before you can use it. You're technically supposed to give it back when you leave town.

Tip 3: Grab any entrance deals you can

Neuschwanstein Castle tickets are virtually never discounted by more than a Euro or two, so unfortunately you're not going to be able to lop much off the advertised prices.

The FüssenCard (above) will offer you a discount of about €2, as will student cards and proof of age for seniors. Combination tickets are also available to visit more than one attraction in Hohenschwangau (see ticketing, on p24, for more).

However, if you're planning on being in Bavaria for a while and want to see a fair few castles, the 14 (consecutive) day **Bavarian Castle Pass** covers you for entry to around 40 different palaces (which includes Neuschwanstein, but frustratingly doesn't include Hohenschwangau Castle).

The ticket costs €24 for an individual or €44 for two adults plus children under 18. This is the best way to save a fair chunk of money if you're sightseeing in Bavaria.

(I should note that there's another variant of the pass: the King's ticket, which offers entry to Neuschwanstein, Linderhof and Herrenchimesee only. It's €24 a ticket, but its advantage is a six month validity - albeit only to those three castles).

Either discount ticket will technically grant you access to Neuschwanstein, but you must be part of a tour to actually enter. The solution to this is to either show your pass at the Hohenschwangau Ticketing Centre, where they'll assign you a tour for free; or to book a tour time online.

If you're choosing to book online, follow the instructions as per the normal tour booking instructions (see Ticketing on p24). The only other thing you need to do is to write a special note in the 'messages' field . Tell them that you have your pass already, and don't need to pay the entrance fee again. Resultantly, they'll then only charge you €1.80 to book the tour time for you.

Some individuals have had success in simply rocking up to the Neuschwanstein entrance gatehouse with the 14 day pass in hand and no tour time booked. There's an office for the Bavarian Palace authority there, and they can technically just waive you onto the next tour for free if you ask nicely. This trick doesn't always work - it's up to you if you'd like to risk it.

More information on purchasing the 14 day ticket is here at http://www.schloesser.bayern.de/englisch/palace/objects/jahresk.htm. You can purchase online at https://www.bsv-shop.bayern.de/index.php?cPath=29 before the trip, if you want.

Tip 4: Bring food

This is definitely not an option for the winter-time, when there's driving snow and you'll need to spend an hour in a restaurant over lunch, just so you can warm up. In addition, it bears saying that food isn't that ostentatiously priced in Hohenschwangau Village - however, drinks, coffee and snacks certainly are.

Even so, you could happily stock up in the local market in Füssen, or at the sandwich shops in Munich station, and take a picnic with you. There're benches and tables a-plenty: many with stunning views.

Tip 5: Consider not going inside Neuschwanstein

A controversial one, but if you're on a very tight budget, you could legitimately consider skipping the interior of the castle altogether - and just enjoy it from a distance (the exterior view is more impressive than the internal rooms, and the guided tour experience can be a little underwhelming).

Some argue - and I'd tend to agree - that the rooms of King Ludwig's Linderhof Palace are more impressive than Neuschwanstein. In addition, the crowds are lighter and entrance is a fraction of the price. However, this option certainly isn't going to be for everyone.

5.2 Saving Money on Rail Travel in Germany

Different trains run on different stretches of German track. These include high speed ICE services, and slower regional trains, which chug to their destination.

It's possible to travel vast distances very cheaply if you're in the know; conversely it's possible to waste vast amounts of money if you don't know the insider track on working the fare system.

So listen carefully!

A Top Tip For Saving Money on German Rail: The Bayern Ticket

If you're going to be spending any time on a train, the Bayern Ticket (Bavarian Ticket) is an essential purchase, and it'll save you a great deal of money. The ticket costs the first person €23, and then €5 extra for each additional person. Up to 5 people total on the same ticket. (If you'd like to use First Class carriages, it's €34.50 for the first person, and then €16.50 for each extra). The ticket is good for one calendar days' travel.

The ticket allows your group unlimited travel on any regional train in Bavaria (those prefixed with codes including IRE, RE, RB, BOB - not long-distance trains, such as IC or ICE). It also includes unlimited travel on buses and public transport - including the metro in Munich and the bus between Füssen and Hohenschwangau Village.

The ticket even includes travel across the Austrian border to Salzburg - an ideal daytrip - so it can literally save you hundreds of Euros if you're with a family.

The only catch is that, on workdays, it's only valid after 9am - so it's not going to be good for an early morning excursion to Neuschwanstein on, say, a working Tuesday. There are no restrictions at weekends or holidays, though.

You can purchase the ticket on any DB ticket machine (look under 'Offers' and then 'Regional Cards'), but it may be easiest to ask for it by name at a staffed counter (this will incur €2 extra charge, but it's tricky to find on a ticket machine).

Your ticket will almost certainly come validated for the present day's use - so you're good to go immediately, and you need do nothing else.

(If you press 'future validation' on the machine, you need to stamp the ticket in a platform-side validator before you start your travel on your chosen day. The purpose of this is so you can buy a ticket for future use, for whatever reason).

An Option For Big Travellers: The Happy Weekend Ticket

Another possibility is the Happy Weekend ticket. It works on the same principle as the Bayern Ticket, but allows you and up to five others unlimited regional train travel, and public transport use, anywhere in Germany (and even into Poland). Evidently, it's only valid on weekends (and either Saturday or Sunday: not both).

It costs €42 for the first person, and €4 for each additional. There's a €2 surcharge if paid at a staffed office.

Because Bavaria's so big, though, and regional trains are pretty slow, you're unlikely to make any real use of this deal - most visitors exclusively use the Bayern ticket, as you probably won't make it across the regional border and back in a day.

A Note About the Bayern Ticket and the Happy Weekend Deal

One quirk of both these deals is that they're not transferable to another person - you can't buy a ticket in the morning and then give it to another family to use in the afternoon.

To prevent transferability, you're meant to write your name on the ticket in the space provided, and then show ID (usually a credit card) when the ticket is checked. In practice, most train guards realise that tourists don't understand the rule, so usually let this pass.

Planning a LOT of train travel?!

If you're going to do a lot of train travel in Germany, you could buy a Bahn Card. These discount cards are really aimed at German residents, but are good for intrepid tourists.

The BahnCard 25 costs €62 and grants the bearer 25% off almost every train fare for an entire year. You'd therefore need to be spending over €250 on rail travel during your trip to benefit from the deal.

The BahnCard 50 costs €255 and, unsurprisingly, grants 50% discount - hence a required rail spend of around €500 before you'd see any benefit.

For completeness' sake, I'm also including the BahnCard 100. It allows you to travel for free on any German train, as much as you please, for an entire year. It's really only a deal for German commuters - for your interest only, it costs around €4,100 a year. (I shudder, as I pay almost that just to get around *London*).

These three BahnCards allow discounted (or free, as in the latter case) travel on high-speed ICE, which isn't included in the other deals. All the cards are purchasable in advance on www.bahn.com.

If You'd Like to Travel on The High Speed (ICE) Trains For Less Money...

If you're not going to be travelling enough to make buying a BahnCard worth it, but you'd like to travel on an ICE train, the best advice is to book your journey as far in advance as you can, at www.bahn.com. Pre-paid fares are much cheaper than walk-up prices on the day - which can easily nudge €100 for a trip between Munich and, say, Stuttgart.

The longer in advance you book, the better the deal. Remember to take ID with you, as ticket inspectors tend to check that the correct person is using a pre-booked ticket.

To Eurail or not to Eurail?

One final note is that, if you're considering buying a Eurail pass (or similar), my advice would be that it's almost certainly not worth it if you're only travelling in Germany - the deals above will save you more.

However, if you're considering visiting other European countries, Eurail passes become potentially more worthwhile. Unfortunately, it's a highly boring job, but it's worth just costing out the price of a pass and the journeys you may make - these passes often don't save you much unless you're banking on doing *a lot* of train travel, so I wouldn't really recommend them.

The Stair Tower, Neuschwanstein Castle

6.0 Where to Stay, Eat and Explore Around Neuschwanstein: Munich

Munich is green, clean and exceedingly wealthy: a stereotype of a perfect German city where everything just seems to tick over with efficiency. It can, however, seem a bit too perfect - everyone seems to ooze money (and it certainly feels like everyone works for BMW).

It's a pleasant place to explore - and millions of tourists do every year. Even so, bear in mind that Germans from elsewhere in the country tend to be a bit disparaging about Munich - it's perceived as being self-satisfied and rather stuck up, and a little time there can reinforce that view.

Even so, it's an interesting place to stay, and lots of tourists attempt a trip to Neuschwanstein from the city.

6.1 Getting From Munich to Neuschwanstein

There are three ways to go about organising a trip from Munich to Neuschwanstein. You can either make your own way there by public transport; you can drive, or you can undertake a guided tour.

Munich to Neuschwanstein on Public Transport

Plenty of tourists do this every day, although do be warned that it's a fairly significant trip.

There are two stages to your journey: first you must catch a train to Füssen from the Deutsche Bahn Hauptbahnhof in Munich, and then you need to catch a public bus from Füssen to Hohenschwangau - the village where the castles are. The train takes about 2hrs, and the bus takes about 15minutes (see the Füssen section on p84 for more).

Trains leave from Munich approximately every hour, and run from platforms 27-36 within the Hauptbahnhof. Half of all trains are direct; the other half require a change at the town of Buchloe. This transfer is extremely quick and easy (unless you've got vast amounts of luggage) and shouldn't put you off taking an indirect train. Note that all trains on this route are little regional puffers, so there are no seat reservations. There are toilets, though.

Tickets during peak time (before 9am) cost €26.70 each way. If you're able to travel off-peak (either during weekends, holidays or after 9am), there are significant discounts available via the Bayern Ticket (see Money Saving, p66).

Alternatively, there are small discounts to booking off-peak tickets online (they're usually discounted down to €22 a leg), but the Bayern Ticket offers much better value.

You can check train times in advance at www.bahn.com. I'd strongly recommend this. If you're prebooking online, you can collect the tickets in person from a staffed counter, or from any DB machine. You need to carry ID with you to use your ticket - it can just be a credit card.

If you're buying a ticket on the day, you can use any DB ticket machine in the station (these all have English options); or purchase from any staffed counter (note that there's a €2 surcharge). Note that 'Füssen' is spelled 'Fuessen' on some of the automatic ticket machines.

Munich to Neuschwanstein by Car

You can drive to Neuschwanstein, although bear in mind that the parking, when you get there, can be a headache in the summer.

The drive is straightforward – leave Munich from the A96 and join the A7 at the first major Autobahn intersection, then follow signs to Füssen/Neuschwanstein once you reach the end of the road. You could comfortably manage the route without a SatNav, although most drivers would prefer one.

There are four carparks in Hohenschwangau (parks are privately owned; cost is about €6 a car). On busy days, the parking lots can fill up and this can pose a headache – you might then need to try and park in Füssen and catch the bus in. There's a largish parking lot by the Füssen train station.

Note that you absolutely can't drive between the castles. Once you've reached Hohenschwangau, you must park and then walk (or take a transit-bus or horse and cart) around the village.

A Guided Trip from Munich To Neuschwanstein

Of course, this is by a long way the easiest option. Many tours will offer their own guide to accompany you for the full day – that includes the castle tour, as well as the transport to and fro – and this can be much more informative than the standard guided tour experience inside Neuschwanstein. You also have someone on hand for tips, questions and queries.

A full guided experience won't be for everyone, but if you're interested, I receive consistently excellent feedback about the agency Viator. They offer an option of different trips which include Neuschwanstein – some are standalone daytrips, and others are multiday excursions to all of Ludwig's castles.

Many trips will pick you up from your hotel, so you don't even need to stay close to the main train station.

For more information these guided tours, have a look at my friend Rita's website: http://www.germany-insider-facts.com/neuschwanstein-castle-germany.html#tours

6.2 Munich Hotels: Where to Stay

Rathaus, Munich

Broadly, if you only want to spend a couple of days in Munich (or you're planning to visit Neuschwanstein on a day-trip), there are two main areas where you should be searching for accommodation: either surrounding the Hauptbahnhof, or in the Altstadt.

Lodging in Munich: Around the Hauptbahnhof

The area surrounding the Hauptbahnhof (that's the main train station) contains most of the cheap and mid-range accommodation, and is by far the most convenient place to stay if you're planning on taking a daytrip on public transport to Neuschwanstein.

There's a real profusion of hotels in this district, most of them mid-range, but with a couple of high-end choices (branches of the luxury Sofitel and Le Meridien chains) directly alongside the main station.

The Sofitel is particularly recommended - it's housed in the old Post Office adjacent to the Hauptbahnhof, and has a character and ambience that's unmatched in the district. The candelit spa in the basement is one of its highlights.

A more reasonably priced choice, where I've stayed in the past, is the Rilano 24/7. It's a little business hotel, albeit with slightly more-stylish-than-average rooms and elaborate mood lighting. There's unfortunately no breakfast room or restaurant: you'll need to find a nearby bakery.

Sofitel Munich

Bayerstrasse 12, 80335 Munich
http://www.sofitel.com/gb/hotel-5413-sofitel-munich-bayerpost/index.shtml
Prices start from €199 a night.

Rilano 24/7 Munich

Schillerstrasse 17, 80336 Munich
http://www.rilano-247-hotel-muenchen-city.de/
Prices start from €59 a night.

The one disadvantage with the Hauptbahnhof district is that the rest of the area (as is typical of the environs of any German train station) is a bit down-at-heel. It's nothing compared to most other European cities, but there's a whole host of depressing looking casinos, shabby ethnic food shops, and busy roads. There are advantages, though - lots of little bakeries to pick up breakfast, and a couple of Aldi and Lidl supermarkets for picnic supplies.

For most visitors, though the most unappetising part is a cluster of table dancing venues - the majority of which are along Schillerstrasse.

To be totally honest, all these things need to be considered in relative terms - things might look shabby compared to the rest of Munich, but it's nothing compared to most of Paris or London. Additionally, although I wouldn't advise you to do anything daft, there's no real concern with crime or safety - it's just a bit grimy.

If you're travelling with a young family or as a single female, you might want to give the area a miss, but for everyone else, it's probably fine - and is extremely convenient.

Lodging in Munich: The Altstadt

The Altstadt (Old Town) is definitely the most atmospheric place to stay in Munich. It's studded with winding streets, the impressive Town Hall, and numerous pretty churches, including the famous church of St Nikolas. Of course, this comes at a price - and, Munich being Munich, the price is somewhat astronomical.

Even so, if you're touring Munich, it's the Altstadt where you'll be spending most of your trip - and so it makes sense to stay here, if the price suits your wallet, and if you don't mind a little journey (about a 15min walk, or a quick metro ride) to the Hauptbahnhof when you want to visit Neuschwanstein (or make any daytrip).

The area contains all the big European hotel chains, including a recommended Mercure - which has all the benefits of a central location without a truly extortionate price.

If you're searching somewhere with a little bit more character, the Cortiina Hotel is modern design hotel with a splash of luxury, literally moments from the Marienplatz and St Peter's Church. The rooftop terrace has a great view of an evening.

Strangely, there aren't any historic hotels in central Munich which I'd really recommend - perhaps due to the city's position as a business destination, most good hotels only really fit the 'clean and modern' bill. If you're looking for antiques and an olde worlde experience, you may need to strike out elsewhere in Bavaria.

Mercure Munchen Central

Senefelderstrasse 9
Ludwigsvorstadt, 80336 Munich
http://www.mercure.com/gb/hotel-0878-mercure-hotel-muenchen-city-center/index.shtml
Prices start from €99 a night.

Hilton Munich City

Rosenheimerstrasse 15
81667 Munich
http://www3.hilton.com/en/hotels/bavaria/hilton-munich-city-MUCCHTW/index.html
It's a a cookie-cutter Hilton, but it's well maintained, central, and reasonably priced (by Munich standards).
Prices start from €149 a night.

Cortiina Hotel

Ledererstrasse 8
80331 Munich
http://www.designhotels.com/cortiina
A design hotel with the German equivalent of *je ne sais quoi*: the location and terrace make it particularly desirable.
Prices start from €199 a night.

Of course, there are plenty of other areas to stay in Munich - you could trek to the East side of the river, or even stay in the cluster of business hotels around the Messe conference centre. Things might seem cheaper, but do realise you're going to have to spend a bit of time commuting on the metro every day to reach Munich's touristy centre.

6.3 Munich Airport Transfers

Munich's international airport is quite a step outside the city - around 50km - but there's no need to worry, as the ever-efficient Germans have got public transport well and truly covered.

The best value (and likely the quickest) way to get to the city centre is on the S-Bahn public transport system. The S-Bahn trains are well signed from everywhere in the airport, and the S1 or S8 line (it doesn't matter which you ride) will drop you at any of the main stations in central Munich, including the Hauptbahnhof.

The journey time from the airport to the city is approximately 45min. Trains don't quite run entirely through the night, but, unless your flight is extremely delayed, they'll be running when you arrive (the transport authority co-ordinates the S-Bahn service hours with the flight scheduling).

The ticket costs €11 one way from the airport to the city. The one tip, if you're intending to tour Munich that same day, is to buy an Airport/City Day Ticket. For only €12.50, the pass will pay for your train journey into the city, and also for all your public transport in Munich for the remainder of that day.

If you're travelling as a group, you can buy a family version of the Airport/City Day Ticket for €23.20.

If you'd prefer to take a taxi from the airport, the cost is around €50 and it'll take about 45min.

If you're hiring a car, you'll find the offices of all the usual firms inside the terminal building.

Snow in Füssen

7.0 Where to Stay, Eat and Explore Around Neuschwanstein: Füssen

Füssen is a picturesque little Bavarian town, close to the border of Austria. It's extremely proud of its Medieval heritage.

Indeed, the town is the final stop on the 350km 'Romantic Road' tourist trail - a route which runs through some of the most picturesque locations in Germany.

(Of course, it could well be the first stop on the trail, depending where you start out!).

Füssen spreads out gently from the river Lech, and the jagged peaks of the Alps form a dramatic (and very visible) backdrop, from pretty much anywhere you stand.

Although Füssen's undoubtedly pretty, its significance on the tourist-trail is mainly due to its proximity to Neuschwanstein and Hohenschwangau. Having said that, there are a couple of attractions in the town which are certainly worth your time.

7.1 Getting from from Füssen to Neuschwanstein

Getting between Füssen and Neuschwanstein is a breeze on public transport. It's a short trip, too, in your own car; although parking can sometimes be a bit tricky.

To reach Neuschwanstein by bus, just catch either bus 73 or 78 - a red bendy bus which starts out immediately adjacent to the train station (across from the ticket office - it's clearly signposted and you cannot miss it).

The buses take about 15min to reach the village of Hohenschwangau, where the two castles are. The buses drop you off at a small tourist information point, where there are toilets.

The ticket office for the castles is a 150m walk from the bus drop-off point. It's effectively just around the corner of the road, although tourists frequently get confused.

Note that the buses aren't super-regular. They come about every 45 minutes during the winter, and about every 25 minutes during the summer. Most up-to-date times are displayed at the bus stops or are available via the Deutsche Bahn journey planner (www.bahn.com).

Bus tickets cost €2.30 single, or €4.50 return. The bus is free with a Füssen Tourist Card, or the Bayern Ticket.

To reach Neuschwanstein by taxi, just hail one of the cream-coloured cabs which circle Füssen or the bus-stop in Hohenschwangau Village (if you can't immediately spot one, there's a taxi phone at the bus-terminus in Hohenschwangau).

Taxi rides are metered. Note that the meter ticks up quickly, and it will be about €15 even for the short, 10km journey. Up to four people can fit into a regular taxi, and a tip isn't expected.

7.2 Things to See and Do in Füssen

The Altstadt

The quaintly-restored town centre of Füssen is an attraction in itself: the cobbled main street runs through a gaggle of pastel-painted timber framed shops, with ample opportunity to buy souvenirs or relax with a beer.

In the wintertime, you can expect a smattering of Christmas market stalls selling decorations and *glühwein*. If you're here in warmer weather, treat yourself to a cherry ice cream at an *eiscafe* - or maybe a *kaffee und kuchen* of a lazy afternoon.

Hohes Schloss & Füssen Art Galleries

The Hohes Schloss (High Palace) dominates the skyline of Füssen, and this little castle is definitely worth your time if you're intending to explore the town.

The first fortifications were laid here way back in Roman times, but the majority of the building work that's visible today took place between 1489 and 1504, when the shell of a fortress (built as a part of the city fortifications) was transformed into a significant late-Gothic castle.

The purpose of the building was part residential, part defensive. As well as a vast banqueting hall, the castle boasted a deep moat and extensive battlements.

You'll find the courtyard of the castle to be particularly interesting, as it's decorated with elaborate trompe-l'oeils - 'trick-of-the-eye' paintings of windows and window-frames, which play with perspective to give the illusion of depth and 3D shape.

The original paintings date from 1499, but note that the paintings visible today have been extensively restored and somewhat re-imagined from the Medieval designs.

As its grandeur would suggest, the Hohes Schloss came to be used as a summer-residence for local religious grandees (the Lord Bishops of Augsburg), but was subsumed into the Bavarian monarchy from 1862, where it became a district court.

In 1931, the Bavarian State Picture Gallery opened within the old bishop's living rooms, and the exhibition today extends to late gothic and Renaissance art from the local region.

There is also an adjoining Municipal Gallery, which displays c19th art.

It's possible to climb the six-floor castle tower (stairs accessed via the State picture gallery), and the views across the town of Füssen are undeniably impressive.

Hohes Schloss and Art Gallery: Entrance Times and Prices

During the winter months (November - March), the castle only opens on Fridays, Saturdays and Sundays.

For the rest of the year it opens every day except Mondays.
Entrance for adults is €6. A combined ticket to use with the local museum is €7.

Allow 1 hour.
http://www.stadt-fuessen.de/hohesschloss.html

St Mang's Basilica and Abbey, and the Füssen Heritage Museum

Adjacent to the Hohes Schloss, you'll discover the baroque extravaganza of the ex-Benedictine Monastery of St Mang. The Füssen Heritage Museum is located the south-western wing of the old abbey, and the adjacent baroque basilica still holds church services. For that reason, you can wander into the small basilica with no entrance charge: to see more of the insides of the abbey, you'll need to cough up the entrance fee to the museum.

The abbey buildings you see were constructed in the early c18th, but the monastery itself dated to the early c9th. It was set up to honour St Magnus, a local recluse who became revered as a Catholic saint.

The reconstruction in the c18th was intended to create a holy palace boasting breathtaking artwork. The architectural style took on lots of inspiration from the adjacent castle - which you can see from the turret-esque outpouchings along its front face.

The monastery once held significant treasures of books and literature, but was dissolved in 1802. Many of its treasures were taken away - shipped down the River Lech in boats.

Today, the Füssen's Heritage Museum encompasses some of the monastery's more impressive baroque halls. In addition, there are seasonal and permanent exhibits, including a display on on lute-making (Füssen was a Medieval hotbed of lute-craft).

Of particular interest is the Ovalbau - an extravagant oval library built into one of the 'turrets' of the front facade. The centre of the room is opened out to allow you to peer down onto the monk's refectory below.

There's an intended architectural link between the need for mental and physical nourishment - contrast the lofty style of the library to the more refined style of the downstairs dining room.

Füssen Heritage Museum: Entrance Times and Prices

Exactly as per the Hohes Schloss, (see above).
Allow around 1-1.5hrs.
http://fuessen-en.ictourismus.de/romantic-soul/the-fuessen-heritage-museum.html

7.3 Hotels in Füssen

Street detail, Füssen

There's a wide selection of hotels in Füssen, and the good news is that they're (by and large) decent quality to boot. Füssen isn't a large place by any means, and most places to stay are located in the town centre. There aren't any big international hotel chains so most hotels tend to be slightly eccentric affairs, run as local family businesses.

The biggest (and most expensive) hotels in the city are studded around the train-station: including the Hotel Sonne; the Hotel Schlosskrone; and the Hotel Hirsch. They're a much-of-a-muchness: all offering good rooms, a vast breakfast buffet, and 4* extras, such as steam-rooms and saunas. I've listed them in order of ascending quality, although they're all safe bets.

Disappointingly, none of the hotels in Füssen are particularly rustic or historic. Although many do have connections to Medieval Füssen, much of their authentic architecture has been overshadowed with over-zealous extensions and conservatories.

Additionally, perhaps in honour of Neushwanstein's overblown decor, the interior design of all four hotels is edging towards the garish. The Hotel Hirsch is definitely the most tasteful of the lot, with the Hotel Schlosskrone's more restrained style coming in a close second.

The Hotel Sonne, although well finished and immaculately cared for, does have an, er, unique aesthetic style which won't be to everyone's taste.

The Hotel Luitpoldpark is closest to the station, and used to be one of the preferred options in town for coach-tours: it's unfortunately getting very tired and is in need of TLC. In its favour, it has a sizeable gym.

Hotel Hirsch

Kaiser-Maximilian-Platz 7 Fuessen, 87629
http://www.hotelfuessen.de/en/
From €125.

Hotel Sonne

Prinzregentenplatz 1 Fuessen, 87629
http://www.hotel-fuessen.de/en/
From €109.

Hotel Schlosskrone

Prinzregentenplatz 2-4 Fuessen, 87629
http://www.schlosskrone.de/
From €109.

Luitpoldpark Hotel

Bahnhofstr. 1-3 Fuessen, 87629
http://www.luitpoldpark-hotel.de/
From €99.

Spatzle with cheese and crispy onions

If you're looking for somewhere a bit cheaper, and a whole lot more rustic, the adorable, family-style hotel Jakob is about 1km from the train station.

It's a little alpine spot, with partially wood-panelled rooms, many of which have balconies overlooking the river Lech. The hanging baskets of flowers probably classify as luxuriant. It's a bit cheaper than the other options, and benefits from a real family feel.

Hotel Jakob

Schwarzerweg 6 Fuessen, 87629
http://www.hotel-jakob.com/
From €69.

8.0 Where to Stay, Eat and Explore Around Neuschwanstein: Hohenschwangau Village

Map of Hohenschwangau Village

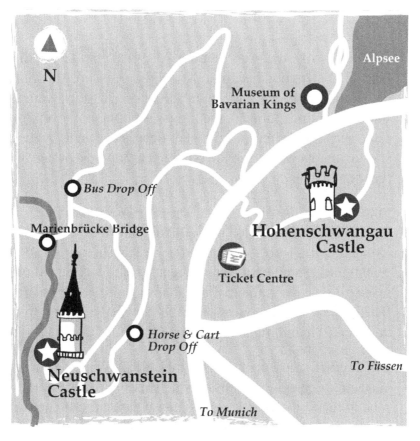

8.1 Things To See And Do in Hohenschwangau Village

Hohenschwangau Castle

Custard-yellow Hohenschwangau Castle sits on the opposite side of the valley to Neuschwanstein. It receives around a quarter of the annual visitors of its younger sibling: a real shame, as it's a beautiful castle in its own right. A visit here affords insight into the mind of King Ludwig - alongside great views of the German Alps.

Quite evidently, the present day castle wasn't built in Medieval times. Construction began in 1833, at the behest of Maximilian II of Bavaria - father of Ludwig. In a fit of eccentricity (which his son would mimic in 1868), the King was hiking in the alps and came across the ruins of a a castle. He was drawn in by the spectacular view, and decided to build a summer-palace here: in the style of a Medieval fortress.

Confusingly, this ruined castle was called *Schwanstein.* Maximilian had stumbled upon the remains of a Medieval fortress founded in the 1300s - although the basic structure had been rebuilt and extended the subsequent 500 years. When Maximilian made his discovery, the castle was in substantial disrepair; but the king was so enamoured with the view that he chose to undertake an ambitious rebuilding project.

In his reconstruction of the building, Maximilian made a number of strange decisions - many of which his son would emulate when rebuilding his own castle, some thirty years later. Rather than employ an architect, he chose a theatre set-designer called Dominik Quaglio. Despite the beauty of Dominik's mock-Medieval plans, he lacked the mathematical and structural skills necessary of a good architect, and the project then cycled through

Hohenschwangau Castle

two other designers.

Building Maximilian's castle was a lengthy process. The king signed-off on designs which emulated the layout of the ruined fortress, but the intricate details (alongside the relative remoteness of the site, and the intemperate weather) meant that construction was a slow process. The majority of the building was finished in ten years; but tweaks and additions were made up until 1855.

The finished castle, however, would have been something of unprecedented beauty (it's just a little overshadowed today). Its interior was equally spectacular. The *pièce de resistance* of the castle - then as now - was the vast mural in the banqueting hall depicting a vast Medieval battle from the Wikina saga. As the tour guides are fond of pointing out, nineteenth century sensibilities mean that there's not a drop of blood painted anywhere on the vast canvas. It was a romantic re-interpretation of the medieval.

To a modern visitor, the rooms of Hohenschwangau Castle are the anthesis of those within Neuschwanstein - the style is cosy, intimate and homely. The ambience is of a comfortable country hunting-home, rather than the cold over-formality of its close neighbour. The rooms are human in scale: the Queen's writing room, decorated with murals of Charlemagne, is fashioned for someone to actually use.

Hohenschwangau was indeed used as a home - albeit only as a hunting-lodge and summer residence for King Maximilian, Queen Marie, and the two little princes Otto and Ludwig. The family spent a couple of weeks here every year: and little Ludwig, left to his own devices, seemed to immerse himself in the ambience of staying in a 'Medieval' castle, whilst his distant father went off to hunt.

It's not hard to see that Hohenschwangau shaped the mind of an impressionable, lonely young boy. In time, Ludwig would begin to adapt the castle to his own passions: installing an unprecedented selection of twinkling fairy lights in his bedroom, emulating the night sky. In time, through a golden telescope (still visible within the fortress), he would peer across the valley at his new castle being built, just in the distance.

Today, entry to Hohenschwangau Castle is organised along the lines of Neuschwanstein: you can only view the interior as part of a guided tour, and tours take place at a time pre-determined on buying your ticket. The upside is that the smaller numbers of visitors means the tours tend to be a little less harried, and conducted in slightly smaller groups. You tend to get about 30minutes in the rooms of the castle, and this is a respectable amount of time to see everything.

Hohenschwangau Castle: Entrance times and prices

These are almost exactly as per Neuschwanstein Castle. See p56 for more.

The Museum of the Bavarian Kings

Placed at a strategic spot at the farthest end of Hohenschwangau Village, in a particularly scenic spot next to the Alpsee, you'll find a modern museum devoted to the lineage of the Bavarian Royal Family.

Most visitors have only ever heard one Bavarian monarch - King Ludwig II himself. However, there were plenty more before him: Ludwig came from an illustrious line of rulers who would otherwise have faded from international consciousness if it wasn't for his eccentric building spree.

The multi-million euro museum is an architectural landmark. From the outside, it's a demure, sophisticated building: but on entering, be prepared to be wowed. The vaulted, cris-crossed ceilings allow glimpses of the surrounding mountains, and glass walled sections afford gorgeous view across the Alpsee. (It's actually won multiple European awards for architecture - the building alone is worth the entrance price).

Inside, the museum is meticulously curated, and balances academia with popular interest to produce something wide wide appeal - from the diehard Ludwig enthusiast to someone with just a passing interest in the young king.

The tragedy is that the museum doesn't yet have the visitor numbers to justify the vast investment. That's a real shame, because it's a really interesting expose on the Wittelbach dynasty, and includes some fascinating artefacts from Ludwig's life.

Most visitors are instantly drawn to Ludwig's ceremonial blue cloak. It's a typically vast, trailing affair, trimmed with fur and feather - as overblown as you might expect. A creative touch is the ability to put on headphones and listen to some of Wagner's work whilst sitting and admiring the vast garment.

The understated parts of the museum are just as interesting. There's a collection of epitaphs to Ludwig, collected from the Bavarian press after he died, giving an interesting perspective on how the king has historically been portrayed in the popular imagination. Included too are advertisements and snippets from guidebooks which lead the first tourists to Ludwig's castles.

The curators understand that most visitors are predominately interested in Ludwig II, and so the lives of other Bavarian kings are somewhat relegated to the sidelines. Even so, there's a fascinating section downstairs on how the Wittlesbach family resisted the Nazi regieme. It's a moving display, particularly as some of the family were imprisoned in concentration camps such as Oranienburg and Dachau.

Museum of the Bavarian Kings: Entrance times and prices

Entrance is €9.50 for adults. Children are free; students and seniors €8.00.

Opening days and times are as per Neuschwanstein Castle.
http://www.bavaria.by/museum-bavarian-kings-hohenschwangau-bavaria

8.2 Walking and Hiking Around Hohenschwangau Village

The Alpine environment around Neuschwanstein is absolutely stunning, and if you're visiting during the summer (or during the milder times of spring or autumn), you could definitely strike out on a couple of walks in the area. They're a good way to get away from the tourist hoardes, and all have great views.

There are three main options, and all are well signposted.

The first route is a circular path around the Alpsee lake. It's evidently a flat route, and you can join it at any point along the lake's edge (most visitors pick up the trail close to the Museum of Bavarian Kings). It's about 5km to circle the lake (around 1.5-2hrs), and there are impressive views across to the castles.

You can also walk a circular route around the smaller Schwansee lake. Access to the Schwansee is slightly less obvious - if you walk to the parking lot near the Bavarian Kings museum, there is a little sign pointing to a footpath, which leads you alongside a stream to the lake itself. It's about 600m along the path to the Schwansee, and circling the lake is only about a 3km walk - so about 1-1.5hrs there and back.

The most ambitious option - albeit with the most impressive views - is scaling the adjacent Mt Tegelberg. Tegelberg is an

Alpine mountain close to the castles, and predictably has great views down onto both Neuschwanstein and Hohenschwangau.

If you make it to the Marienbrücke Bridge, there's a path leading on from here up the mountain. It's a pretty steep climb to the top, and it's likely to take you 3 hours - definitely come with suitable shoes and equipment, as this is something for experienced walkers rather than just daytrippers.

It's not a particularly easy walk, although the big advantage is there is a transit system which runs up the other side of the mountain - which means that, if you make it to the top, you can catch the cable car back down the other side (the terminus is a quick taxi ride, or a couple of kilometres walk, from Füssen).

The better option, in my opinion, is to take the transit system up, and then walk down the mountain to the Marienbrücke. It's still a tricky walk, but it's mainly downhill that way. It should take you about 2 hours.

More information about the Tegelberg Cable Car is at http://www.tegelbergbahn.de/. A nice bonus is that the ride is free if you've a Füssen discount card.

If you're after a less ambitious summer activity, you can get out in a boat on the Alpsee. There's a variety of crafts for hire, from paddle-boats to rowing boats, all equipped with vast safety jackets.

The boat-house is clearly signposted from the end of the village, near to the Museum of Bavarian Kings. Boats can be rented from the half hour, upwards.

8.3 Hotels in Hohenschwangau Village

As I've said before, there's nothing like staying in Hohenschwangau Village to really transform your experience of visiting Neuschwanstein Castle. Although lodging options are predictably pricey, they represent good value for money.

There's one stand-out hotel in the village, and that's the Hotel Müller. The Müller family have had links to Hohenschwangau Village since 1690, ascending to wealth from their horse-drawn carriage transportation business. They were lucky enough to be in the right place, in the right time - their little guesthouse alongside the trade-route blossomed as tourists began to flock to Neuschwanstein.

Hotel Müller is open seasonally, and boasts a highly recommended restaurant (see my section on eating, below), alongside some of the cutest rooms in the whole of the village. Most of the simple accommodations come with wood-panelled walls and pretty checked quilts, but visitors really come for the view from the bay windows or terraces: an interrupted vista of either Hohenschwangau Castle or Neuschwanstein itself.

The hotel provides a vast, generous breakfast to set you up for the day; and horse and cart rides to Neuschwanstein depart from directly outside the hotel.

The hotel enjoys rave-reviews from other travellers on TripAdvisor. I'd really recommend you to take a look at it.

Hotel Müller

Alpseestrasse 16, 87645 Hohenschwangau
http://www.hotelmueller.com/
Prices start from €115 a night.

8.4 Eating in Hohenschwangau Village

Be warned that snacks, drinks and souvenirs in Hohenschwangau Village are extremely expensive. Full table service meals are, proportionately at least, somewhat more reasonable, although the quality is very variable.

The best place for either a quick lunch or a more casual evening meal is undoubtedly the Hotel Müller - which is also the best place to stay in the village.

The wooden panelled dining room offers either a quick-service menu for lunchtimes (bratwurst, sandwiches or pasta served in literally minutes), or a more leisurely lunch or evening meal, with Bavarian classics for around €13-16 a main.

Contact details are as per the accommodation section, above.

The best reviewed restaurant in Hohenschwangau is the 'Alpenrosen Am See' - a fine-dining experience in a modern setting, attached to the Museum of Bavarian Kings. There's a phenomenal view across the adjoining Alpsee lake from the restaurant terrace, and there's nowhere more romantic when the sun is setting.

The menu balances traditional Bavarian fayre - saddle of venison with nut butter, for example - alongside more modern dishes, such as mango rice with duck drumstick and chorizo. The restaurant holds 'historic' nights around once a month - with traditional food and a themed dining experience to commemorate, say, the birthday of Wagner.

Mains are in the region of €25-€35. There's no desperate need to reserve, except on themed nights and in the high season.

Alpenrosen Am See Restaurant

Alpseestrasse 27
87645 Hohenschwangau
http://www.hohenschwangau.de/1114.0.html

A Final Note

Thanks very much for buying this guide.

If you've enjoyed it or found it useful, it'd mean a huge amount to me if you could leave a review on Amazon. Your review makes a significant difference, and I'd really appreciate a few seconds of your time to leave some comments for others.

If you've any further questions about Neuschwanstein, visit exploring-castles.com and click 'contact me'. I'll try my best to help you out. If you feel I've missed out on anything, or if you've any tips you'd like to share in a future edition, I'd love to hear from you.

Likewise, if you're interested in castles, history, or exploring Europe, please do check out exploring-castles.com. It's full of photos and stories from castles all around the world.

I've also a coffee-table print book, 'Exploring English Castles', which you might enjoy. (See below).

Thanks again for reading. Have an incredible trip to Neuschwanstein.

Enjoyed This? Then Begin Exploring English Castles....

- Do you know what lies in Merlin's Cave, deep beneath Tintagel Castle?

- Why a brutal murder of an archbishop drove King Henry II to build Dover Castle?

- Or how King John captured Rochester Castle using the explosive might of big, fat, pigs?

English castles are steeped in thousands of years of intrigue. They're home to devious plots, and incredible legends.

After years of research, I've uncovered some of the most amazing tales from English castles...

..and, with a little help from a publisher in New York, I've created a beautiful new book about them.

Exploring English Castles is a 10x10.5" coffee table book. It contains more than 200 full colour photographs of some of the most beautiful castles in England.

You'll also find fascinating floor-plans of nine of the most interesting English castles, to help you visualise the fortresses as they once were.

Booklist, of the American Library Association, endorsed **Exploring English Castles** with a great review:

"This big, luscious book ushers the reader over Great Britain...

....For each of the castles, the author provides a 'snapshot of one of the most notable moments in [their] past,' such as a royal visit or a particularly significant siege, by which is not only the castle's story told but also major occasions in British history. For travelers as well as history buffs."

You can buy your copy of Exploring English Castles through any good book retailer in the USA, Canada, Australia or Europe. Retailers include Amazon, who stock hard-copy and also Kindle editions.

Praise for 'Exploring English Castles':

"An exquisite book!" Natalie Grueninger, historical researcher and writer of *In The Footsteps of Anne Boleyn*

"Dr Morris brings history alive and evokes such a sense of place and vibrancy," [5* Review, Amazon.com]

"I wish that this book had been published two years ago, before my family and I traveled to England,"[5* Review, Amazon.com]

"It is a book I will refer back to for years to come and proudly display on my bookshelf," [5* Review, Amazon.ca]

Made in United States
North Haven, CT
24 November 2022

27198169R00059